"*Just Think* is a book that offers up the wisdom of the ages along with the Nancy Nordenson's encouraging spin on living life thoughtfully in the here and now. It's a book I recommend to anyone who believes life is not just for existing, but also for growing with the gifts we've been given!"

—Joan Steffend, television host

"A page-turner is a book that holds the attention and motivates a reader to whip through page after page with bated breath. It's usually associated with 'fast' reading. Nordenson's book is in a rare class of 'slow' page-turners. So rich with quotations from many sources and her own finely crafted aphorisms and analogies, her pages make me want to 'just think' for a while yet hasten on to find the next treasures. Here is an excellent mind worth following as closely as you can and sentences worth pondering as long as you can."

—Doug Newton, senior editor, *Light and Life Magazine;* executive director, Free Methodist Communications

"*Just Think* is a lovely, lyrical book that calls us to 'think in order to live more abundantly.' Nancy Nordenson writes for all women of faith, including those with little formal education. Her book provides invaluable guidance on a host of topics: how to grow in wisdom, how to see and appreciate beauty, how to balance faith and reason, and how to become equipped for creativity. Her insights will help readers live life more richly and worship God more fully."

—Katherine Kersten, senior fellow of the Center of the American Experiment, columnist, Minneapolis *StarTribune,* writer, past commentator on MPR

"Nancy Nordenson joyfully invites us to dust off our mental cobwebs and open our minds and hearts to new possibilities for living and thinking. Nothing is mundane or ordinary in Nancy's world. A used airline ticket stub, family photos, rocks, and shells are among the familiar objects in a busy day that become taking-off points for her thoughtful reflections on life's big questions. She gently nudges us into our own fresh world of mental and spiritual growth and guides us along the way to become wiser in leading lives of significance and service."

—Donna Erickson, executive producer and host of PBS' "Donna's Day" and author of *Fabulous Funstuff for Families.*

"This could become a little classic of practical spirituality for women. Long on wisdom, compassion, and insight, *Just Think* is a delight to read and ponder."

—Victoria Moran, author of *Creating a Charmed Life*

"Well written and practical, *Just Think* is an invitation to think big. It's a compelling call to fully engage your mind in order to fully embrace life. A must read for everyone."

—Dr. Kevin Leman, psychologist and author of *The New Birth Order Book*

JUST THINK

NOURISH YOUR MIND TO FEED YOUR SOUL

NANCY J. NORDENSON

Baker Books
A Division of Baker Book House Co
Grand Rapids, Michigan 49516

Published by Baker Books
a division of Baker Book House Company
P.O. Box 6287, Grand Rapids, MI 49516-6287
www.bakerbooks.com

Printed in the United States of America

Library of Congress Cataloging-in-Publication Data
Nordenson, Nancy J., 1957–
    Just think : nourish your mind to feed your soul / Nancy J. Nordenson.
        p.   cm.
    Includes bibliographical references.
    ISBN 0-8010-6456-2 (pbk.)
    1. Christian women—Religious life. 2. Thought and thinking—Religious aspects—Christianity. I. Title.
BV4527.N65 2004
248.8′43—dc22   2003017275

To David, Erick, and Alex—my joy here and now
To Catherine—my joy yet to come

CONTENTS

ACKNOWLEDGMENTS

Writing is an inherently solitary endeavor. Yet by God's grace, my efforts have been fueled and sustained by a number of benefactors: Friends who encouraged me in conversation or over e-mail, on walks or over coffee, through flowers or cards. Friends who respected the privacy of a manuscript in progress yet graciously read it when asked. Friends who prayed for me or asked, "How's the book coming?" with expectant smiles on their faces or in their voices. A bookstore owner who gave me a prophetic word about this project when we had never before met. A work colleague who, while on a bus from Breckenridge to Denver, challenged me to take this project from the abstract to the concrete and make it happen. Teachers of the Christian faith who opened my eyes and mind and heart wider and wider. Parents whose love and care helped set the trajectory of my life, which early on established the path that would lead to this book, and whose generous words of early review sealed it with a blessing. My husband and sons, who enveloped my solitary work with love, patience, unwavering belief, and many kindnesses. God, the ultimate benefactor, who sets his purposes in motion and never fails to work together for good the circumstances—whether of pain or pleasure—in my life.

INTRODUCTION

As a young girl, I often stood in my mother's pink gingham–wallpapered kitchen pondering a cartoon taped to the refrigerator. "Mommy, why did you go to college?" asked one of Bil Keane's *Family Circus* children in a cartoon published decades ago. The querying child addressed his exhausted mother as she stood in the kitchen, pressed upon by the accoutrement of her daily life—baskets of laundry, stacks of dirty dishes, toy-covered floor. I asked my mother, probably equally exhausted and standing at the sink, "Why is this funny?" She told me that someday I would understand.

Why do I remember this cartoon so clearly more than thirty years, a college degree, two children and a husband, a full résumé, and countless loads of laundry later?

The cartoon worried me. As a young girl, I loved school and dreamed of college. I thought that learning was one of the good things in life, indeed, that it was *for* life. It worried me that learning and thinking might be disconnected from being a grown-up, from real life. Was that the big secret my mother thought life would fill me in on later?

As an adult, I join my mother and the *Family Circus* mother in the dailiness of real life. At home, my mind is filled by the activities of the everyday: making sure that those in my household have food to eat, clean clothes to wear, transportation, and routine dental exams. At work, my mind is bought and paid for by clients that expect its full attention. Keeping up at home and at work is enough to consume my mind from the time I wake up until I go to bed.

I am a woman and my business is to hold things together.[1]

F. Scott Fitzgerald, *Tender Is the Night*

I suspect that I'm not alone. Many women's minds are probably similarly consumed by the demands of the day: the young mother with three children under the age of four, the forty-five-year-old divorcée navigating a new life, the executive swept from one meeting to the next. Many of us are left with little time or energy for thoughts of a richer variety: ideas, dreams, plans, questions, meditation, contemplation, study. Thoughts that feed our souls and make us grow, that bring us closer to wisdom. Instead, our thoughts are increasingly narrowed to the needs of our most routine days. The challenge of moving through each day anchors minds otherwise designed to soar.

Yet is that the way it is supposed to be? In adulthood we have our most important work to do. In *The Mature Mind*, H. A. Overstreet wrote, "Adulthood . . . is the significant period toward which life heads. It is the time when all the preparings can come to their fruition."[2] As adults, our thoughts now shape the futures of our families, communities, schools, churches, governments. Whether we're in a corporate boardroom, factory, or kitchen, what we do now will impact generations to come. How can we shoulder these responsibilities with minds anchored only to routine, to the tasks of the everyday? How can we launch the future on an exciting trajectory unless we're growing, learning, dreaming, and becoming wiser?

The secret behind the *Family Circus* cartoon may well be that learning and thinking are terribly disconnected from being a grown-up, from daily life.

Yet I have another idea.

The secret of the cartoon may actually be deeper and far more satisfactory to the idealistic young girl still inside me. Perhaps the secret lies in what I couldn't see, in what the *Family Circus* mother did when she wasn't being caricatured by Mr. Keane. Perhaps I couldn't see all the ways the *Family Circus* mother was working, without her children's knowledge, to keep her mind fresh and strong. The *Family Circus* children probably were not aware of the books she read before bed, or the writing she did to record her days, or the extent to which she prepared for a class she taught. Nor could they see the way she challenged her thoughts to test truth and integrity. They didn't know how hard she tried to find time for ideas and dreams and contemplation.

Any kind of women, and any kind of work. Each day I have one woman on with me—a dancer, a housewife, whatever—and I ask her about what she does. You'd be amazed how much wisdom women have that they didn't know they had.[3]

Faith Sullivan, *The Cape Ann*

"Any kind of women" (and any kind of men) has enormous potential for thought. Each one of us has been blessed and entrusted with a magnificent mind that we get to use

13

every day. And we get to use it not just to make it through each day, but to thrive. To fold each day into a life that is rich and expansive. Having such a mind to use is a gift from God; using it well is a gift back to God. *Just Think* is about increasing the vision and expectations of how we can use our minds in and beyond our everyday lives.

In the pages that follow, you won't learn how to get smarter in thirty days or read ten tips for a better memory. You won't deepen your knowledge of cognition or learning theories, or discuss the faculty of reason with ancient Greek philosophers. Instead, we'll explore habits and strategies we can weave into our days to employ our minds to the fullest and to ensure that we are mentally ready for the possibilities adulthood holds for us. To clarify the link to real life, story lines from real and fictitious characters are interwoven. And importantly, I'll use teachings of the Christian church and Scripture. A discussion of the life of the mind can be entire only within the context of the Creator of the mind.

I offer the following readings to you not because they represent anything new and undiscovered. After all, it's probably true that there is nothing new under the sun. Rather, I hope you may find it helpful to see a range of ideas and strategies laid out in one place—like having all the pieces of a jigsaw puzzle facing up when the puzzle is begun. Although the puzzle can most certainly be completed with some pieces up and some down, or even with all the pieces down, the task is easier and more efficient when all the pieces can be surveyed, reminding the player of all she has to work with.

As you read, may your magnificent mind be enlivened and your soul of immeasurable worth be enriched.

1

A MIND FOR LIFE

A Mind in Love with God

A teacher of the law asked Jesus: "Of all the commandments, which is the most important?"

Jesus answered: "Love the Lord your God with all your
heart and with all your soul and with all your mind and
with all your strength." [1]

I wonder: What does it mean to love God with all my
mind?

I understand what it means "to love with all my heart."
That concept and phrase is used often in regard to spouses,
lovers, and children. But who says to a loved one, "I love
you with all my mind"? What does it mean to love God
in that way?

Consider these possibilities:

The mind in love with God is intellectually pleased and satisfied with God. There is a mental "click" when God is regarded. The mind's energy resonates with God's. Instruction, questions, and contemplations related to God are welcomed, entertained, and enjoyed. Dorothy L. Sayers, creator of the Lord Peter Wimsey detective series and Christian theologian, referred to the intellectual channel through which she loved God as the "passionate intellect."[2]

The mind in love with God is engaged with God's thoughts and ways, just as a lover is engaged with the words and actions of the beloved. The engaged mind wants to learn God's ways, to imitate the elegance of his mind, to study his creation, to please him in its use. It seeks the habits of mind that Jesus emulated—study and teaching; the use of questions, metaphor, and story; the knowledge of history, Scripture, and culture; the practice of prayer and solitude; and the blending of faith and reason, heart and mind.

But we have the mind of Christ.[3]

From the Book of 1 Corinthians

The mind in love with God has knowledge of God. It is difficult, if not impossible, to love someone or something of which you have no knowledge. The Early American theologian Jonathan Edwards said, "There can be no love without knowledge . . . The reasons which induce the soul to love, must first be understood before they can leave a reasonable influence on the heart."[4] God's character, the revealed hints about the nature of his existence and relationship with humankind, as well as his creation and the history of his involvement with it, impress the mind as something worthy to be esteemed and pursued.

The mind in love with God is enlivened, just as we come to life when in love. Alert to the greatness of God, the mind seeks synchrony with that greatness. Contrary to the popular opinion that one's intellect declines under the influence of divine allegiance, the mind in love with God expands to a greater range of thought. Not only does it seek to absorb the greatness to which it is now alert, but it also desires to focus on the fine detail of that greatness, not unlike the way the Creator emphasized exquisite detail as the foundation of an expansive universe.

Mr. Emerson's religious convictions were at the center of all his instruction. He believed that every act of the mind could and should contribute to the greater glory of God. Every proposition in logic, every chemistry equation, every law of physics rightly understood was a demonstration of the goodness of God and the impetus to right action.[5]

Elizabeth Alden Green, *Mary Lyon and Mount Holyoke*

The mind in love with God is sensitive to serving God, just as a husband and wife are sensitive to opportunities to serve each other. Such a sensitized mind volunteers itself to be put to use for God. It is eager to receive and be filled; it is generous to give back and be used.

The mind in love with God is focused on God, the divine object of its love. "Fix your thoughts on Jesus," says the writer of the Book of Hebrews.[6] Thomas Kelly describes a simultaneous focus on daily life and the divine: "On one level we may be thinking, discussing, seeing, calculating, meeting all the demands of external affairs. But deep within, behind the scenes, at a profounder level, we may also be in prayer and adoration, song and worship and a gentle receptiveness to divine breathings."[7]

The mind in love with God courts the guidance of the source of knowledge and wisdom. It recognizes the connection between thought and prayer and unites them: "God, be in my mind and hear my prayers. Know my thoughts. Feed me yours—put them in my mind. I'm thinking."

. . . for Christ is a Word that does not give voice to the ear but goes directly into the mind.[8]

Ron Hansen, *Mariette in Ecstasy*

A Matter of Integrity

As I looked, I felt more profoundly impressed than ever with the mystery of that unknown something which may be named "vital spark" . . . whose absence or presence makes all the immeasurable difference, between an inert mass of matter . . . and . . . a living brain, by whose silent and subtle machinery, a world may be ruled. [9]

This observation was made by a young doctor, Edward Curtis, who while participating in an autopsy held a brain in his hand—Abraham Lincoln's brain. The same brain in which the Presidential Oath of Office was contemplated and affirmed, in which countless agonizing decisions were made regarding the course of the Civil War, in which the meaning and mandate of freedom for all was translated into the words of the Emancipation Proclamation.

I am fearfully and wonderfully made.[10]

From the Book of Psalms

Thought emerges from the "silent and subtle machinery" housed behind our eyes and between our ears, from waves of biochemicals washing over billions of nerve cells embedded in roughly three pounds of spongy gray matter. How it emerges is a mystery. Especially considering that while this three-pound organ is weaving contemplations, decisions, and language, it is at the same time causing one's heart to beat, expanding the lungs to receive air, sensing thirst, welcoming sleep, and controlling virtually every function necessary for life.

Nancy's brain was in a whirl.[11]

Carolyn Keene, *The Mystery of the 99 Steps*

Thought is not produced by the brain in the same manner as tears are produced by the glands just under the eye or blood by cells deep inside bone. The brain is the loom on which are strung threads of experience, knowledge, and emotion. To think is to weave those threads. Like any process in which raw materials are transformed into a product, thinking can be done carelessly or artistically. It is our choice. We aren't limited by our intelligence, only by the desire and will to do the best we can.

Consider this: A woman who performs brain surgery for a living would likely score higher on a test that measures intelligence than would most women who don't perform brain surgery. But would the brain surgeon necessarily score higher on a test that could measure how carefully she applies her mind to all of life—from the daily minutiae to the issues that count for eternity? The answer is no. We all have the capability to score equally high on such a test,

19

despite the fact that some may be "smarter" than others. In fact, might not a high score be expected of each of us?

> *But John Woodrow was twenty-six, and not a thing going for him but his looks. I might could say he had brains working for him, but he put his smarts to such a bad use that I wouldn't feel right calling him intelligent.*[12]
>
> Kaye Gibbons, *A Virtuous Woman*

Each of us has power and influence over more things or people than we might count at first thought. Each of us is like a gear that turns other gears, which turn untold numbers of other gears. While intangible in itself, thought gives rise to decisions, judgments, dreams, plans, beliefs, and solutions with tangible effect on our personal and corporate worlds, just as Lincoln's thoughts had a profound effect on our nation and world. To wield that power or influence with integrity, we must think well.

Is it reasonable that others should trust our judgments and decisions? Is it reasonable for others to assume that careful thought preceded our actions? Is it reasonable for others to expect that a foundation of substance underlies our words, "I think that . . ."? Should one's soul expect that one's mind has considered and reflected on matters of truth and faith before advising that in unison they take the stand, "I believe . . ." or "I don't believe . . ."?

Thought in the Realm of Abundance

The list of things an average woman might have to think about in a single week's time is long and varied. Here is an excerpt from a hypothetical list: Get ready for overnight guests, strategize how to pay a large bill, care for aging parents, plan menus, manage a chronic disease, file insurance forms, deal with a family divorce, write a letter to a bank, carry out a project at work, solve a problem with a neighbor, get stains out of laundry, teach a class, attend a committee meeting, decide on a discipline strategy for a child, make a grocery list, and arrange for a mechanic to fix the car and a plumber to fix the pipes.

This list illustrates a first tier of thinking I'll call "thinking in order to live." This tier includes thinking that is necessary to accomplish what we need to accomplish on a somewhat daily basis. The second tier of thinking I'll call "thinking in order to live abundantly." Although seemingly a luxury, this tier is actually a necessity to living life in a manner in which we dream dreams, reach and accomplish, ponder and evaluate beliefs, search for answers to questions, and focus on thoughts that bring joy. These two tiers of thought can occur simultaneously, but it may be more likely that the second tier is free to take place only when the first is able to be set aside.

Naturally, the merry Christmas bringing the happy New Year, when fellow-citizens expect to be paid for the trouble and goods they have smilingly bestowed on their neighbours, had so tightened the pressure of sordid cares on Lydgate's mind that is was hardly possible for him to think unbrokenly of any other subject . . . But he was now a prey to that worst irritation which arises not simply from annoyances, but from the second consciousness underlying those annoyances, of wasted energy and a degrading preoccupation, which was the reverse of all his former purposes. "This is what I am

thinking of; and that is what I might have been thinking of,"
was the bitter incessant murmur within him, making every
difficulty a double goad to impatience.[13]

George Eliot, *Middlemarch*

"Thought constitutes man's greatness," said Pascal,[14] but it can't, I would add, if it is focused solely on immediate daily demands and concerns. If our thoughts are consumed with what we need to do to get through our days or weeks, no room is left for the thoughts about what we can and need to do with our lives. Thinking well and clearly about the many daily issues within our realms of responsibility allows these issues to be more readily resolved, leaving mental space and energy for thoughts of a higher realm—those that constitute abundant life and result in vision, opportunity, hope, or creation.

Principle of Return

Pair extravagance with the work of the mind. That is Annie Dillard's attitude when she writes,

One of the few things I know about writing is this: spend it all, shoot it, play it, lose it, all, right away, every time. Do not hoard what seems good for a later place . . . These things fill from behind, from beneath like well water. Similarly, the impulse to keep to yourself what you have learned is not only shameful, it is destructive. Anything you do not give freely and abundantly becomes lost to you. You open your safe and find ashes.[15]

The suggestion of such an extravagant expenditure of thought, however, triggers a natural leeriness. Somehow it seems prudent to hold something back, as if the mind's present contents and abilities need to last a considerable length of time, as if the mind subsists on a fixed income of thought and its earning power has no possibility of increase or decrease.

It is not hard, however, to expose the fallacy of this frugal approach to mental expenditure. Think back to a period in which you let your mind sit untouched. Consider the weakened mental ability and forgotten ideas that probably followed such a period. Next, remember a period in which you were actively and vigorously thinking and consider the mental re-invigoration that followed. The contrast of mental outcomes—weakened ability and forgotten ideas compared with mental re-invigoration—should demonstrate that the frugal approach is as poor a plan as living only on money placed once upon a time under a mattress.

Herzog smiled at this earlier avatar of his life . . . Herzog the man on whom the world depended for certain intellectual work, to change history, to influence the development of civilization. Several boxes of stale paper under his bed in Philadelphia were going to produce this very significant result.[16]

Saul Bellow, *Herzog*

Jesus told the following story: A man going on a journey entrusted his money to his servants during his absence. He distributed the money according to each servant's ability. To one servant, he gave five talents of money, to another two, and to another one. The servant to whom five talents had been given put them to work and earned five more. The servant to whom two had been given did the same thing, earning back two talents on the work of the original two.

But the servant who had received only one talent hid the money in the ground.

When the man returned from his journey, he checked on his money. To the servant who had made five talents from his original five, the man said, "Well done." Likewise, to the servant who had made two talents from the two he had been given. The man rewarded both servants' faithfulness over a few things with a promise of charge over many. But what of the servant with the buried single talent? In anger over the talent's lost potential gains, the man took the single talent from the miserly servant and gave it to the servant who now had ten talents. "For everyone who has will be given more, and he will have an abundance. Whoever does not have, even what he has will be taken from him." [17]

Henry David Thoreau directly applied the moral of this story to thought. "The Scripture rule, 'Unto him that hath shall be given,' is true of composition. The more you have thought and written on a given theme, the more you can still write. Thought breeds thought. It grows under your hands." [18] It is like the word game in which one has to find as many words as possible using the letters of someone's name or a holiday or a slogan. (For example: Think of all the words you can create using only the letters found in "Christmas.") At first it seems difficult to find more than a few two- or three-letter words. Then, as one's mind starts working on the directive, an amazing number of words begin to come to mind.

Similarly, once your mind is applied to the thought written on its internal blackboard, new thoughts emerge: If this, then that; I remember so and so . . . ; This reminds me of . . . ; I must learn more about . . . ; I wonder why . . . ; What does this mean?; Does this have anything to do with . . . ? The initial thought on even the driest subject can become the capital for a rich mine of thought as your applied mind drills down to a fertile vein.

Courting a Powerful Thought

Once upon a time, a new thought—of the powerful variety—visited a young woman's head. Whether it was divinely placed or arose out of her recent mental labors is still a matter of dispute among those who knew her. But what is not a matter of dispute is this: Her life was never the same afterward.

In past years, the young woman had heard stories from travelers visiting her village about thoughts that were powerful enough to change the direction of one's life. What's more, these travelers reported that other people's lives had also shifted course because of what that powerful thought had brought about in the one it had originally visited. Hunger was satisfied, diseases healed, poverty lifted, difficulty eased, loneliness comforted, joy restored, lives transformed.

She wanted such a story to be true about her as well. She became consumed with the question, What is possible for me? The young woman offered up her mind to God as a vessel in which a vision might be placed.

I longed to tell her about that feeling I'd had of some special mission to perform. But I can't lay my fingers on what the mission is yet.[19]

Catherine Marshall, *Christy*

And so she began to court her thoughts, often writing them down in secret, hoping that she would find just one

25

of the powerful variety, no matter how small. She prayed to God, she talked to those in the village who could boast of great adventure, she read the poetry of those who had tasted great sadness. She watched. She waited.

Then one night it happened. Where before had been only the thoughts she knew so well, now was born a new thought, a thought of power, a thought with vision and possibility. And that thought loomed large in her mind.

All the young woman's thoughts began to attend to that large and powerful thought, like servants attending a visiting queen, as if they recognized that indeed this was a thought of a higher order. All of the young woman's energy, which until now had gone into seeking, now surged forward with potency, carving out of rock a riverbed in the direction her life would now move.

As she lived with this thought in the days that followed its visitation, she knew it would stay with her, that it had been given to her. She had been granted what she had asked and what she had sought: a powerful thought. With fear and gratitude she summoned the courage to ask God, as Mary had asked the angel, "Let it be as you have said."

And she set about the work the powerful thought required of her.

2

THE NEEDED BALANCE

Of Faith and Reason

I believe certain things to be true because I can figure them out. Other things I believe to be true despite the fact that I can't completely figure them out. In the first case, my belief is based on reason. In the second case, on faith. Pope John Paul II writes, "Faith and reason are like two wings on which the human spirit rises to the contemplation of truth . . ."[1]

Thought arising from reason, however, can have a tendency to remain falsely separate from thought arising from faith. Like layers of a cake held together loosely by icing in the middle, they are apt to slide apart with the right provocation. Reflection—rolling a thought around over and over, thinking long and hard about something—helps to hold these slippery thoughts together more securely, helps to blend thoughts of reason and faith together into integrated lines of thought. Reflection allows the food metaphor to change from layering a cake to seasoning soup. A little more salt, a little more garlic; a little more faith, a little more reason. Back and forth, blending. Back and forth, asking, Do I have it right yet?

Reflection lets us remove reason and faith from their respective vacuums and place each in the context of the other. Reason is examined against the backdrop of faith; faith is examined by the light of reason. We can then ask, How does this reasoning reflect faith? How does this faith reflect reason?

Picture a scale with two stainless-steel weighing plates suspended from a crossbar by chains on either side of a center pole. The steel plate holding the heavier object falls, while the plate holding the lighter object swings up, suspended in air. In my mind's eye, I can load all my faith on one side and reason on the other. Does the reason side fly up as the faith side crashes down? Reflection gives me pause to ask why. Why does my God-given reason not match my God-given faith? Or the reverse: The faith side swings in the air as the reason side falls heavily to the table. Again, why? Reflection helps me look at what is filling the fallen side and missing from the suspended side.

My goal is to have as much faith as its stainless-steel plate can hold and as much reason as its plate can hold. Both sides packed down, stacked up, towering, solid. Both plates, faith and reason, hanging in perfect balance.

Of Mind and Heart

The practice of thinking to our fullest capacity does not mean that we disregard our hearts, any more than loving our families and friends means that we disregard our minds. We don't choose one or the other—mind versus heart; we choose both.

Consider the example of Mary after the birth of Jesus: "Mary treasured up all these things and *pondered them in her heart*" (emphasis added).[2] To ponder means to weigh carefully in the mind, to reflect, to meditate. To link this mental activity with the activity of the heart, as Mary did, is to use our best parts in combination rather than exclusion.

We who are created in the image of God can look to God and Jesus for vivid examples of the tension needed between mind and heart, intellect and emotion. For example, God "founded the world by his wisdom and stretched out the heavens by his understanding"[3] yet he tells us, "I have loved you with an everlasting love."[4] Jesus taught, prayed, and asked probing questions, yet he wept, grieved, and longed to gather Jerusalem's children "as a hen gathers her chicks under her wings."[5] He told his followers to be "as shrewd as snakes and as innocent as doves."[6] Martin Luther King Jr. expanded on this idea in *Strength to Love:* "To have serpentlike qualities devoid of dovelike qualities is to be passionless, mean, and selfish. To have dovelike without serpentlike qualities is to be sentimental, anemic, and aimless. We must combine strongly marked antitheses."[7] Mind and heart—we must not use one without the other.

In the short story "Ethan Brand,"[8] Nathaniel Hawthorne tells the story of a fictitious lime-burner who goes in search of the "Unpardonable Sin," the "only crime for which Heaven could afford no mercy."[9] After eighteen years, he found what he had sought: the exaltation of mind at the expense of heart.

"It is a sin that grew within my own breast," reported Ethan Brand to his listeners, "The sin of an intellect that triumphed over the sense of brotherhood with man, and reverence for God, and sacrificed everything to its own mighty claims!"[10]

Thus Ethan Brand became a fiend. He began to be so from the moment that his moral nature had ceased to keep the pace of improvement with his intellect.[11]

Nathaniel Hawthorne, "Ethan Brand"

Extreme intellectual pursuits destroyed the balance between heart and mind. Brand had raised himself to the highest pinnacle of intellectual achievement. "But where was the heart?" wrote Hawthorne. "That indeed, had withered—had contracted—had hardened—had perished. It had ceased to partake of the universal throb."[12]

3

FORWARD MOVEMENT

I Was Younger Yesterday

I was younger in 1986.

I look now at a picture taken that year of me and my husband, bright and smiling against a background of blue sky and white sand. Between us our two-year-old firstborn child is standing on a ledge that is waist-high to me. He is leaning into my shoulder. My arm cradles him; his father's arm guards him from behind. His father wears a proud smile.

How young we were in those early years of our first child's life.

If my husband and I had been shown at that moment the immense amount of growth that life would require of us in the years to come, would we have been able to stand so assuredly and smile so confidently? Such an unobscured vision of the future might be likened to looking ahead to the last problems in a math textbook during the first day of class. Previewing one's academic future in that way never failed to bring disbelief that the challenges ahead would be possible to meet. Nonetheless, as the class progressed, one gained assurance as chapter after chapter led toward solving that final problem.

Life is like math class. Through the mercy of life's design we are spared receiving a lifelong body of knowledge and experience all at once. Instead, life offers its learning opportunities day by day, masked in disguises trivial or profound—as work or play, joy or sorrow, success or failure.

"I see it now," she said presently. "It is very strange to say one is young at the moment one is speaking. But to-morrow I shall be older. And then I shall say I was young to-day. You are quite right. This is great wisdom you are bringing, O Piebald Man." [1]

C. S. Lewis, *Perelandra*

We learn from our experiences as we go through them, and also as we look back on them. When looking back, we can reflect on those experiences from an older and hopefully wiser perspective, even if we're older by just one day. Like the island woman in C. S. Lewis's *Perelandra*, we can accept yesterday and today's inevitable naiveté with calm and humility, and look with gratitude and optimism to a new day in which to be older.

Every day we'll have been young. Every day we'll be older.

Moving to What's Next

Journal entries that sound the same page after page. Conversations with a déjà vu quality. Unsolved problems, repeated regrets. Circuitous stalled thought. Inertia. I can yawn with boredom or sigh with frustration at these symptoms. Or I can heed their warning: My thoughts are not moving forward—which means that *I* am not moving forward.

I'd planned to take my aunt away from him, and see justice done, and then, when it was all over, to find work on a farm somewhere . . . But now I can't look ahead any more; I can't make plans or think for myself; I go round and round in a trap, all because of a man I despise, who has nothing to do with my brain or my understanding.[2]

Daphne du Maurier, *Jamaica Inn*

In all our thinking, our intention must be to move forward. Often, thinking a thought to the next reasonable step is sufficient to maintain sustained forward movement. Not all matters, however, are this straightforward. For many issues, moving forward can arise only from long periods of thinking or brooding and rarely occurs as a straight uninterrupted shot. Sustained movement in these cases more likely resembles a three-dimensional spiral that starts at point A, then rises and moves toward point B as it simultaneously appears to backtrack and lose altitude and momentum. The apparent losses may be due to changing ideas, new information, new insights, reexamination of facts, or even a readjustment of what point B actually is. What is important, however, is that one's will continue to be directed forward, toward point B. Just as a car tends to travel in the same direction as the eyes of the driver, so thoughts travel in the direction of the will.

To move forward, guard against moving backward. Monitor the trajectory of your thoughts, particularly those three-dimensional spiraling thoughts. As a brick kicked behind a tire keeps it from rolling backward, so a physical reminder of mental movement keeps thoughts from rolling backward. A record of decisions or notes of a train of thought are helpful physical reminders of the hard work already finished in a thinking process. Like a bread-crumb trail, these reminders also help monitor and document the upward spiral. Remembering where you started helps you see how far you've come.

No, Katie never fumbled. When she used her beautifully-shaped but worn-looking hands, she used them with surety, whether it was to put a broken flower into a tumbler of water with one true gesture, or to wring out a scrub cloth with one decisive motion—the right hand turning in, and the left out, simultaneously. When she spoke, she spoke truly with the plain right words. And her thoughts walked in a clear uncompromising line.[3]

Betty Smith, *A Tree Grows in Brooklyn*

Lives and thoughts characterized by forward movement are marks of mature, growing individuals. Sometimes, however, only time can confirm a forward direction. Oswald Chambers suggests, "Compare this week in your spiritual history with the same week last year and see how God has called you up higher."[4]

Evidence of the Journey

The back of my plane ticket stub reads, "This portion of the ticket should be retained as evidence of your journey." Unexpected wisdom courtesy of a commercial airline. This same mind-set is shared by grade-school teachers. Every June during my children's grade-school years, their teachers sent them home for the summer with portfolios under their arms, the folders bulging with routine math papers and spelling tests, as well as special poems, booklets, and artwork. Viewing their accumulated work of the past year, in one place and at one sitting, their progress was unmistakable. While day-by-day growth in knowledge, understanding, and proficiency was hard to detect, the growth over a nine-month period was always startling. This annual viewing of the portfolio brought not only a "Wow!" from my lips as I recognized their progress, but a sense of "Yes, I did that!" from theirs as they were reminded of all they had done.

As adults, we also need that sense of "Yes, I did that!" or any variation on that theme—"I learned that!" "I made it through that!" The expanse of our lives is evident when we are reminded of the journey through our days by a picture, a song, a smell, a journal entry. Or when we recall our "firsts"—first love, heartbreak, job interview, home. Or when we relive in our minds a series of days that were difficult or joyful or ordinary. By revisiting the evidence of our journeys, we remind ourselves that we are more than what we are at any one moment.

Mightn't it be a good thing if everyone had to draw a map of his own mind—say, once every five years? With the chief towns marked, and the arterial roads he was constructing

from one idea to another, and all the lovely and abandoned
by-lanes that he never went down, because the farms they led
to were all empty?[5]

Charles Williams, *The Place of the Lion*

I am usually pleased to remember that I am more than what I am at any particular moment. In rather dull and predictable moments, I am gratified to be reminded of days of success and excitement. In moments of success, I am grounded when reminded of days of work that preceded the success. In any moment, I am humbled and reassured when reminded of the workings of God in past days of my life, and enriched when I recall past lessons learned.

The problem is that it is too easy to forget the days of success and excitement, to forget the hours of work, to forget the times that God has acted, to forget lessons learned—even when I think all of it is seared into my brain.

To remember, the journey must be intentionally marked. A journal, a collection of old songs, personal mementos, a bottle of old perfume, newspaper clippings, special books, family photographs, notes of books read, a work portfolio, a list of important dates. These factual and sensory reminders help bring the map of your life journey onto your mental desktop.

So much of the past is encapsulated in the odds and ends.
Most of us discard more information about ourselves than
we ever care to preserve. Our recollection of the past is
not simply distorted by our faulty perception of events
remembered but skewed by those forgotten. The memory is
like orbiting twin stars, one visible, one dark, the trajectory

of what's evident forever affected by the gravity of what's concealed.[6]

Sue Grafton, *"O" Is for Outlaw*

When you have saved the evidence of your journey, you are free to access it. You are free to remember yourself as a young person, to reappreciate the sorrows you've endured and the joys you've treasured, to take what you learned yesterday and bring it forward to today. All of your past remembrances can help shape who you are today, can help you be the multidimensional person time and experience have made you.

Take the advice of the commercial airline and follow the example of grade-school teachers. Gather and save the evidence of your journey so you can reconnect with who you've been and what you've lived. Mark your journey as you go. Markers of the journey illuminate what has passed and point toward the way ahead.

Prepared Paths

The manner in which we think each day eventually becomes the manner in which we habitually think. Well-worn mental paths are more easily traveled than new unbroken terrain. These paths are to one's benefit when they have been formed through careful thought; they are detrimental when formed otherwise.

A positive mental path, or habit, keeps mental energy channeled toward progress. Days filled with thinking and doing, entwined with yesterday's thinking and doing, not only improve the present but eventually bear future and long-term fruit and accomplishment. For instance, laboriously practicing piano scales today improves the likelihood of a favorable performance at next week's piano lesson, but it also lays the foundation in the fingers, as well as in the mind, for future successful recitals. Today's habits may result in tomorrow's parenting breakthrough, or next year's art, or next decade's published book.

She kept her eyes on this door and tried to recall lessons learned in other venues, other vocations. [7]

Joan Didion, *The Last Thing He Wanted*

As even the trace of an abandoned path through the woods remains evident enough to show the way, so abilities developed and ideas explored are never wasted, even if they are never fully or directly utilized. For example, the mental paths blazed while learning trigonometry in high school or reading a difficult book last year increase one's capacity to navigate more easily and effectively other intellectual endeavors at any time in the future.

Data from the acclaimed Nun Study support this. Dr. David Snowdon studied cognitive function in a group of 678 nuns from seven convents in six states over a period of more than fifteen years. [8] Autobiographies written by a subset of seventy-four nuns while in their twenties were a key source of data. [9] Snowdon found that the denser with ideas was a nun's early autobiography, the better her cognitive function late in life.

Ideas you've generated, ways in which you've thought, and things about which you've learned all help cut paths in your mind and form mental habits, enabling you to conquer that which you have yet to think and learn about. What has been prepares the way for what is yet to come.

38

Leaving Ignorance Behind

Do you not know?

Have you not heard?[10]

From the Book of Isaiah

Jesus turned to those to whom he had given himself in teaching and asked, "Do you still not understand?"[11] The disappointment in that question is unmistakable. Is there also impatience, weariness, sadness? How many times has that same question left divine lips to fall unwelcome on my ears?

I can imagine the original recipients of Jesus' question may have bristled at the insinuation of ignorance and slowness, at the intentional inducement of guilt. I may have been tempted to counter: Consider all that I do know and understand; isn't it enough?

Yet the reality is that I understand far less than I think I do.

In the reception area where I waited, all the magazines were work-related, copies of Pit & Quarry, Rock Products, Concrete Journal, and the Asphalt Contractor. A quick glance was sufficient to convince me that there were issues at stake here I never dreamed about . . . My, my, my. Sometimes I marveled at the depths of my ignorance.[12]

Sue Grafton, "M" Is for Malice

When I stop shining the light on what I claim to know and understand, and dare to shine it on what I don't, awareness of my personal ignorance is awakened. Ironically, awareness that I am ignorant about much more than previously thought is progress. Just as a defense lawyer needs to discover what he doesn't know about the prosecutor's case in order to go about the work of defending his client, so I need to discover what I don't know in order to go about the work of my life.

We all have work to be about—children to raise, jobs to carry out, degrees to complete, changes to effect, problems to solve, relationships to maximize or restore, beliefs to name, people to serve. We have truths to discover, meaning to realize, joy to claim, justice and mercy to mete out, holiness to live, God to worship, and on and on. All this requires a foundation and growing storehouse of knowledge and understanding.

The commitment to leave ignorance behind begins by becoming aware of our personal ignorance and then facing it without flinching. Once that reality is faced, we can identify the areas of ignorance that are unacceptable in light of the work we must be about. (Although all of us don't need to abolish the same areas of ignorance—for example, I don't need to understand quantum physics—there are areas of ignorance we all must abolish. Jonathan Edwards said, "You are all called to be Christians, and this is your profession. Endeavor, therefore, to acquire knowledge in things which pertain to your profession."[13]) Finally, those identified areas of ignorance should be reduced by intentionally increasing relevant knowledge and understanding.

For myself, I don't want to reach eighty years of age and then realize that I could have done or was supposed to do such and such, but due to ignorance I was never ready. I don't want to find I missed anything because I "still [did] not understand."

Methinks that in looking at things spiritual, we are too much like oysters observing the sun through the water, and thinking that thick water the thinnest of air.[14]

Herman Melville, *Moby Dick*

4

BREADTH OF LIFE,
FULLNESS OF THOUGHT

The Well-Stocked Mind

The universe offers an almost unlimited inventory from which we stock our minds. And we stock them from that inventory either by intentional choice or by default through the vacuum approach, in which material of all or any variety is pulled in randomly to fill the void.

Whatever is true, whatever is noble, whatever is
right, whatever is pure, whatever is lovely, whatever is

admirable—if anything is excellent or praiseworthy—think about such things.[1]

From the Book of Philippians

Obviously, the better method of stocking the mind is through intentional choice, which is the only method that allows worthy and valuable content to be selected. We need such content for all the following reasons and more:

- To be catalyzed, expanded, and ignited. Those of us who have battled a blah spirit and lifeless mind on one or more occasions won't find it difficult to draw a link between the state of our spirit and the state of our mind. (At such times, an enlightened question to ask is, What have I been thinking about today?)

- To stay optimistic and not lose hope or vibrancy. The world is full of wonderful things.

- To link reason and imagination. To see the chasm between what is and what could be. To see possibility. To detect opportunities for greatness.

- To know the richness, vastness, and beauty of that which has been divinely created.

- To form a solid foundation from which to launch action.

- To provide sufficient mental content of beauty and joy so that we are less likely to gravitate toward content of despair or fear.

- To be equipped for creativity. To gather raw materials to be assembled and shaped at some future date.

- To have a sense of the existing body of knowledge and to add to that body. To continually chop away at the immense amount we don't know or understand.

- To be prepared. We can't predict what we'll need to know or when we'll need to know it. Knowing how to ride the "El" in Chicago enables one to more easily navigate the metro in Paris. Nothing is wasted.

We did A Passage to India *as a set book when I was at school. I used to think it overrated. But no knowledge is wasted in police work, as they used to tell me at training school, not even E. M. Forster apparently.*[2]

P. D. James, *The Skull Beneath the Skin*

A mind stocked with experience, information, insights, and knowledge of high caliber has a rich and dense mental inventory from which to catalyze thought, build knowledge, and take action.

Consider All This

So much world exists beyond the walls of my kitchen, my home, my office. Knowledge extends almost infinitely beyond what I learned in my college major, beyond what is reflected in my city's newspaper or favorite magazines. The full import of ideas developed over the ages represents a universe of thought most of us leave largely unexplored during our days of routine living. We have more things to think, wonder, and learn about than any of us could ever list or even imagine.

Consider the Library of Congress book classification system.[3] Twenty-one general topic categories expand into over two hundred subcategories. To tantalize your brain with the

potential cognitive feast at its disposal, read through this
partial list of subcategories:

Philosophy
Logic
Psychology
Aesthetics
Ethics
Religions
Mythology
Judaism
Christianity
The Bible
Theology (doctrinal
  and practical)
Auxiliary sciences of
  history
History of civilization
Archaeology
Diplomatics
Archives
Seals
Numismatics
Inscriptions
Epigraphy
Heraldry
Geneology
Biography
Geography
Mathematical geog-
  raphy
Cartography
Physical geography
Oceanography
Environmental sci-
  ences
Human ecology
Anthropogeography
Anthropology
Folklore
Manners and customs
Recreation
Leisure
Social sciences
Statistics
Economic theory

Demography
Economic history and
  conditions
Industries
Land use
Labor
Transportation
Communication
Commerce
Finance
Sociology
Social history and
  conditions
Social problems
Social reform
The family
Marriage
Societies
Communities
Classes
Races
Social pathology
Social and public
  welfare
Criminology
Socialism
Communism
Anarchism
Political science
Political theory
Political institutions
  and public adminis-
  tration
Local and municipal
  government
Colonies and coloniza-
  tion
Emigration and immi-
  gration
International law
International relations
Law of the Roman
  Catholic church

Theory and practice of
  education
Music
Visual arts
Architecture
Sculpture
Drawing
Design
Illustration
Painting
Print media
Decorative arts
Philology
Mathematics
Astronomy
Physics
Chemistry
Geology
Natural history
Biology
Botany
Zoology
Human anatomy
Physiology
Microbiology
Medicine
Pathology
Internal medicine
Surgery
Ophthalmology
Otorhinolaryngology
Gynecology and
  obstetrics
Pediatrics
Dentistry
Dermatology
Therapeutics
Pharmacology
Pharmacy
Nursing
Homeopathy
Agriculture
Plant culture

45

Forestry	Building construction	Photography
Animal culture	Electronics	Manufacturing
Aquaculture	Aeronautics	Handicrafts
Hunting sports	Astronautics	Home economics
Engineering	Chemical technology	Military science

This list of things to think, wonder, and learn about doesn't even mention the more than 220 countries listed in my edition of the *New York Public Library Desk Reference*. Each with its own history, political structure, folklore, language or unique blend of languages, body of literature or oral tradition, industry and resources, and religious customs. Neither does this list include the fifty states within the United States, each with its own distinct culture. Or the many topics that for the sake of space were left out.

In the academic world, groupings of knowledge are referred to as domains. Just like the name implies, each domain is its own little world with unique facts, vocabulary, experts, history, and even ways of thinking, asking questions, and discovering more knowledge. So the breadth of things it is possible to think, wonder, and learn about actually extends not just to all the possible topics, but to specific ways of thinking, talking, and discovering more about each of those topics.

Look at what a lot of things there are to learn . . . You can learn anatomy in a lifetime, natural history in three, literature in six. And then, after you have exhausted a million lifetimes in biology and medicine and theocriticism and geography and history and economics—why, you can start to make a cartwheel out of the appropriate wood, or spend fifty years learning to begin to beat your adversary at fencing.

After that you can start again on mathematics, until it is time to learn to plough.[4]

T. H. White, *The Once and Future King*

In addition to the above listed topics, or domains, there is a lifetime of ideas or concepts to examine and think about. The first two volumes of the multivolume *Great Books of the Western World* published by Encyclopedia Britannica hold discussions of 102 "Great Ideas" or concepts.[5] These two volumes together are called the "Syntopicon." The 102 ideas are subdivided into 3,020 topics. The discussions refer the reader to everything that has been written about each topic in the 517 works contained in the *Great Books* series.

Consider all there might be to think, wonder, and learn about these ideas or concepts from the "Syntopicon":

Angel	Emotion	Labor
Animal	Eternity	Language
Aristocracy	Evolution	Law
Art	Experience	Liberty
Astronomy	Family	Life and death
Beauty	Fate	Logic
Being	Form	Love
Cause	God	Man
Chance	Good and evil	Mathematics
Change	Government	Matter
Citizen	Habit	Mechanics
Constitution	Happiness	Medicine
Courage	History	Memory
Custom	Honor	and imagination
and convention	Hypothesis	Metaphysics
Definition	Idea	Mind
Democracy	Immortality	Monarchy
Desire	Induction	Nature
Dialectic	Infinity	Necessity
Duty	Judgment	and contingency
Education	Justice	Oligarchy
Element	Knowledge	One and Many

Opinion	Relation	Temperance
Philosophy	Religion	Theology
Physics	Revolution	Time
Pleasure and pain	Rhetoric	Truth
Poetry	Same and other	Tyranny
Principle	Science	Universal
Progress	Sense	and particular
Prophecy	Sign and symbol	Virtue and vice
Prudence	Sin	War and peace
Punishment	Slavery	Wealth
Quality	Soul	Will
Quantity	Space	Wisdom
Reasoning	State	World

The lives of great people consitute another dimension of the breadth of things to think, wonder, and learn about. Headlines from the worlds of politics, sports, and entertainment introduce us to popular or significant figures, but they can't begin to populate our minds with as many lives of interest and meaning as can the rich biographies of saints and explorers and scientists and patriots. By studying the lives of great men and women, we can see examples of how the above topics and ideas intersected with a range of human personalities, passions, and journeys throughout the course of history.

A World Too Small

The travel ads on the pages of the *New Yorker* show a large and lovely world. My world is small in comparison. I spent my early childhood in a northern city on the Mississippi River, and I came of age in a southern city on the Gulf of Mexico. Today I live one block from a creek that feeds into the Mississippi that feeds into the Gulf. My mind has woven its vision of the world on the warp and woof of those 17 degrees of latitude and 11 degrees of longitude.

But what patterns, colors, and textures might be found in the other 163 and 349 degrees, respectively, by which my tapestry could be enriched and expanded?

Rebecca: I never told you about that letter Jane Crofut got from her minister when she was sick. He wrote Jane a letter and on the envelope the address was like this: It said: Jane Crofut; The Crofut Farm; Grover's Corners; Sutton County; New Hampshire; United States of America.

George: What's funny about that?

Rebecca: But listen, it's not finished: the United States of America; Continent of North America; Western Hemisphere; the Earth; the Solar System; the Universe; the Mind of God—that's what it said on the envelope.[6]

Thornton Wilder, *Our Town*

Limited venue is just one factor contributing to a too-small vision of one's world. Seventeenth-century philosopher John Locke expanded on these factors when he proposed "why some men of study and thought, that reason right, and are lovers of truth, do make no great advances in their discoveries of it":

The reason whereof is, they converse with but one sort of men, they read but one sort of books, they will not come in the hearing but of one sort of notions: the truth is they canton out to themselves a little Goshen, in the intellectual world, where light shines, and as they conclude, day blesses them; but the rest of that vast *expansum* they give up to night and darkness, and so avoid coming near it. They have a pretty traffic with known correspondents, in some little creek; within that they confine themselves and are dextrous managers enough of the wares and products of that corner, with which they content themselves, but will not venture out into the great ocean of knowledge, to survey the riches that nature hath stored other parts with, no less genuine, no less solid, no less useful, than what has fallen to their lot, in the admired plenty and sufficiency of their own little spot, which to them contains whatsoever is good in the universe.[7]

Many of us (including this author) have developed one or more unconscious "rules" by which we confine ourselves to the "admired plenty and sufficiency of [our] own little spot," keeping our worlds comfortably small. For example:

- Limit reading to one subject, one genre, or one author or type of author (with that type being the one that most closely resembles oneself).

- Avoid the opinion-editorial page of the newspaper on which various views from many people from many walks of life are recorded, or alternatively, read only one's favorite columnist or the piece with the headline most closely aligned to one's own view.

- Be content to travel only to tried and true locations that feel like home. Consult a map only to find out how to get to a destination by the fastest, most direct route. Disregard all the space and names of towns that do not lie on that route.

- Hold at a distance new friends and acquaintances who have different ways of doing and thinking about things.

- When choosing between two activities, make the choice based on personal comfort and the likelihood of satisfaction.

- Limit historical interest to the years from one's birth to the present.
- Stop a conversation before it gets to a point at which there may be disagreement.
- Have the mind-set of being finished. Finished learning, discovering, judging, and deciding.

These examples underline how unnecessarily we limit our world. Although we may long to know a bigger world, how many of our actions continue to reinforce a smaller one?

For a naturalist, traveling into unfamiliar territory is like turning a kaleidoscope ninety degrees. Suddenly, the colors and pieces of glass find a fresh arrangement. The light shifts, and you enter a new landscape.[8]

Terry Tempest Williams, *An Unspoken Hunger*

Enlarging your world is like living in one room your whole life and knowing every corner, every inch of it—the way the morning light comes in the east window, the cracks in the wall, the way the furniture is placed just so, the trick to opening the flue in the fireplace, the light lift that an afternoon breeze gives the curtains—and thinking that of all the rooms in all the world, how wonderful it is that you know and have this room. Then suddenly a hidden door opens, and just adjacent to your well-used and familiar room, you see another room grander than you ever knew existed—with colors in combinations you've never seen, windows that catch the light from all directions, and furniture such as you've never imagined. And you see all this simply by going from what is familiar and loved to what is unfamiliar yet worthy to be explored and embraced.

51

In the Game

A commercial for a "reality" television program made this offer to potential viewers: "They live; you watch." Those words should knock you between the eyes and force a rebellious "No!" from your gut.

Henry Adams would have posthumously joined in the rejection of this offer to live vicariously through others. Adams, grandson of President John Quincy Adams and great-grandson of President John Adams, admitted to being born into the game of life with an "excellent hand." Yet in his later years, he mourned the choices he had made by which he learned of life only in a passive, vicarious manner. Writing of himself (in the third person) in *The Education of Henry Adams:* "As it happened, he never got to the point of playing the game at all; he lost himself in the study of it . . ."[9]

Don't you know most of the people in the world are not individuals at all? They never have an individual idea or experience? . . . They get their most personal experiences out of novels and plays. Everything is second-hand with them. Why, you couldn't live like that.[10]

Willa Cather, *The Song of the Lark*

If you wanted to learn about trains and went about it by reading a stack of books about trains, you could learn a great deal. You could learn how the tracks were laid and by whom. You could learn how the engine is fueled and how it moves the train. You could learn what education train engineers need, and the differences between a traditional train and a monorail train.

But unless you traveled by train, you couldn't learn a number of things: the smell inside the train car; the feel of the upholstery; the gentle rocking as the train speeds along; the sound of the whistle as the train moves through a crossing; the sight of people at a small town station waiting either to board or to greet disembarking friends or family; the way your body tips and sways when moving between two cars and the surety of step such a transfer requires; the sensation of riding high above the ground, of appearing to sail over rivers and highways.

Similarly, you could learn about looking for a job from a stack of books. The books would tell you how to write a résumé, how to prepare for an interview, and which industries and companies to approach with your type of expertise.

But until you actually write a résumé, you won't discover the difficulty, and satisfaction, of assigning words to your past experience. Until you've gone through an interview, you won't feel the strain in your back that comes from sitting up oh-so-straight while an interview stretches on. You won't know how tricky it is to find out about the future employer when it is the future employer who is guiding the interview. Until you pursue a job, you won't know the agony of a letter that says, "Thank you for your interest, but . . ." or the elation of a late-day telephone call extending a job offer. You won't appreciate the dilemma of knowing whether to say yes or no.

Two things everybody's got tuh do fuh theyselves. They got tuh go tuh God, and they got tuh find out about livin' fuh theyselves."

Zora Neale Hurston, *Their Eyes Were Watching God*

Assertively embrace life to learn from it for yourself. Live and be filled with sensations of touch and sound and color. Learn from life in order to live more fully. Only by actively living can you achieve the three-dimensional reality of sensory information, head knowledge, and gut feeling.

As Iron Sharpens Iron

As iron sharpens iron,

so one [person] sharpens another.[12]

From the Book of Proverbs

Eleanor Roosevelt lacked a formal education. Concerned about her perceived deficiency, she made a game of learning by talking with people. She wrote, "After awhile I had acquired a certain technique for picking their brains. It was not only great fun but I began to get an insight into many subjects I could not possibly have learned about in any other way. And, best of all, I discovered vast fields of knowledge and experience that I had hardly guessed existed."[13]

Southern novelist Flannery O'Connor once confided to a friend that she wished someone "real intelligent" would write to her. A woman, "A," wrote to her soon after, beginning a correspondence that lasted nine years, until O'Connor's early death. Among the things O'Connor and "A" discussed in their letters were books each was reading; issues of faith, belief, and church doctrine; current projects and accompanying struggles; and opinions and counteropinions. They often exchanged articles and books via mail for later comment or discussion. O'Connor told her friend and correspondent, "Your writing me forces me to clarify what I think on various subjects or at least to think on various subjects and is all to my good and to my pleasure."[14]

How dull my mind has grown. It was wonderful to sharpen it against her awareness.[5]

Anne Morrow Lindbergh, *The Flower and the Nettle*

British authors Charles Williams, C. S. Lewis, and J. R. R. Tolkien met every Thursday evening in a group they called the Inklings. In addition to reading their writing to one another, Inklings members passionately discussed and argued. Each was stretched by the knowledge the others possessed. About the importance of such interaction, Williams wrote, "Much was possible to a man in solitude, but some things were possible only to a man in companionship . . ." And about his Inklings friends, he wrote, "They are good for my mind."[16]

I want the likes of Eleanor Roosevelt, Flannery O'Connor, and the Inklings group in my life, passionate thinking people who will hold me to a high standard of thought and mental energy. I want my mind grabbed by dialogue that soars above the necessary small talk of socially mandated meetings. Dialogue that will introduce me to places and ideas I need to encounter. I want those whose hearts and minds I trust to correct me, question me, challenge me, astonish me.

"I have a great deal to say, but it isn't recipes, and that's all the women at home ever talk about. Cooking and sewing and their children and family matters."

"It's practically all they talk about here."

"If you say something that's an idea," Nora said, "they look at you as if you'd just gone out of your mind. They actually get embarrassed and after a minute or two start talking about something else."[7]

William Maxwell, *Time Will Darken It*

Following the example of Roosevelt, we can expand and deepen our thought life via interested and enthusiastic conversation. We can be prepared to meet people with questions and thoughts of our own to share. We can learn what others are doing, thinking about, and reading and find out where they've been and where they're going. Following the example of O'Connor, we can sharpen our iron via written correspondence. We can borrow some lines from her correspondence:

- I am wondering if you have read . . .
- From what I have read about that, I think . . .
- In my opinion . . .
- I can never agree with you that . . .
- I wonder why you convict me of . . .
- I am learning to . . .
- I hope I have not left you with the impression that . . .
- I have an interesting article on . . .
- On the purely spiritual side, I refer you to . . .
- I got interested in . . .
- What I was thinking about was . . .
- I suppose when I say . . . I mean . . .
- The enclosed says where my thought heads on the subject of . . .
- What you say about . . . now brings it home to me . . .
- I've always believed . . .
- I continue to think that . . .
- Would you be interested in reading . . . ?[18]

Following the example of Williams, Lewis, and Tolkien, we can form a community of thinkers who discuss and challenge one another. Sharing not only our ideas but our work. Learning from one another not just about what we think but how we think.

Eyes Wide Open

Thomas Jefferson's Monticello home, nestled in the hills of Virginia, is dense with beauty and history. I visited Monticello one summer with my family. Our tour group included a large three-generation family. Before the tour began, the grandfather of this family passed out new pocket-sized spiral notebooks (green, red, blue, purple, yellow) to every family member, young and old alike, keeping one for himself. Then he gave instructions for a contest: Write down every fact you discover. The winner is the person who discovers and records the most facts not discovered or recorded by anyone else.

The tour—and contest—began. Ears listened; eyes looked; hands scribbled. Even those of the grandparents. Faces lit with joy when private discoveries were realized.

This grandfather showed his family the spirit of a wide-eyed student of life: Open your eyes; look around; see what you can discover!

Son of man, look with your eyes and hear with your ears and pay attention to everything I am going to show you, for that is why you have been brought here.[19]

From the Book of Ezekiel

When we open our eyes, one thing we can't avoid seeing is nature—a common object of observation and, therefore, a common venue for discovery. Ralph Waldo Emerson wrote in his essay "The American Scholar," "Every day, the sun; and, after sunset, Night and her stars. Ever the winds blow; ever the grass grows. Every day, men and women, conversing—beholding and beholden. *The scholar is he of all men whom this spectacle most engages*" (emphasis added).[20] In a similar vein, the Old Testament psalmist continually calls our attention to nature in numerous variations of the same theme: "The heavens declare the glory of God; the skies proclaim the work of his hands. Day after day they pour forth speech; night after night they display knowledge."[21]

A fig tree was the object of one of Jesus' lessons.[22] Observe, he urged. What lesson can be learned from the changing moon? Or a spider web? What can the amazing and orderly growth and development of a child teach you? What does the symmetry of hair swirls on animals or of chromosomes lined up inside dividing cells reveal about the elegance of creation and the Creator's mind?

Nurse Rooke . . . is a shrewd, intelligent, sensible woman. Hers is a line for seeing human nature; and she has a fund of good sense and observation which, as a companion, make her infinitely superior to thousands of those who, having only received "the best education in the world," know nothing worth attending to.[23]

Jane Austen, *Persuasion*

"People watching," particularly of those close to home, is a dividend-rich application of observation skills. Look often into the eyes of those you love. Watch how they hold their coffee cup. Notice the food they push around their plate. Don't miss their eagerness or reticence to talk at the breakfast table. Waiting for your next bus or plane, watch the people waiting with you. Wonder about the stories of their lives.

Be alert to the culture around you. Pay attention to clothing and hairstyles. Acquaint your ear to the strains of music, the sounds of traffic, the din of people in public places. Note the books people are reading, the headlines in magazines. Listen to church bells and ask yourself why they ring.

What do you see? What do you hear? What can you learn from it all?

The Books by Your Bed

"Isn't it wonderful what Oprah has done for reading in this country?" a woman asked the bookseller as she inspected the selections displayed on the Oprah Book Club table.

The bookseller seemed troubled by her comment. "Yes," he said as he lifted his eyes and scanned his store, "but there are a lot more good books than just those Oprah recommends."

In fact, nearly 2 million books have been published in the United States since 1980 and another 1.3 million between 1880 and 1980.[24] With this number of choices, even the most voracious reader reads only a tiny fraction of what is available.

Let's suppose the woman I observed in the bookstore reads one book every month for fifty years of her adult life. Add a few for vacation weeks; subtract a few for weeks with too much work or sick children. The sum of this equation is a bibliography of five hundred to seven hundred books. These books and their ideas will help shape her adult life.

The question: Will she abrogate the choice of these books to Oprah, a monthly mail-order book club, or the *New York Times Book Review*, or will she, in the words of Virginia Woolf, let her mind look over the bookshelf, "as it chooses and rejects, making itself a dwelling-place in accordance with its own appetites"?[25]

Think back to the last time you stood in a library or bookstore surveying a row of books. What titles delighted you? What words caused your eye to linger? The titles that delighted you are probably not the same titles that would delight your neighbor. Your eyes lingered on words the woman next to you quickly passed over.

If the woman I observed in the bookstore does not discover the titles on which her eyes linger, but instead limits her reading to only books recommended to her by experts and celebrities and others who have no knowledge of her life, she may never discover her interest in the survival stories of pioneer women, or fall in love with the writing of an obscure British novelist, or realize she has a craving for theological essays, or find that 1948 out-of-print volume whose ideas will change her life.

"It's the books and paintings I want to look at. H'm! Books, you know, Charles, are like lobster-shells. We surround ourselves with 'em and then we grow out of 'em, and leave 'em behind, as evidence of our earlier stages of development."[26]

Dorothy L. Sayers, *The Unpleasantness at the Bellona Club*

As Lord Peter Wimsey, mystery writer Dorothy L. Sayers's aristocratic detective, suggests, a stack of books can provide valuable clues about the reader's life. The stacks of books by your bed or on top of your desk should be unlike anyone else's stacks. The matrix of thoughts represented by your independent selections can't be duplicated by any other individual.

If someone were to study the stacks of books by your bed, would the evidence reflect your life or Oprah's?

5

ACCOMMODATIONS FOR THOUGHT

Of Kitchen Sinks and Fire Escapes

The cool tranquil silence of the library envelops those working here—the retired gentleman reading the paper, the young woman with the baseball hat hunched over her open books, the boy mumbling to himself as he walks along the rows of books dragging his hand as he goes. There are others here, all on assignment, all with some reason to be here on an afternoon.

Did they inhale the luxurious aroma of books, as I did, when they walked through the door? Did their souls and minds quicken, as mine did? Is the silence—broken only by the staccato of short coughs, computer beeps, and turning pages—as inspiring to them as it is to me?

Where do your mind and soul quicken? Where can you go to think?

I write this sitting in the kitchen sink. That is, my feet are in it; the rest of me is on the draining board, which I have padded with our dog's blanket and the tea-cosy. I can't say that I am really comfortable, and there is a depressing smell of carbolic soap, but this is the only part of the kitchen where there is any daylight left. And I have found that sitting in a place where you have never sat before can be inspiring—I wrote my very best poem while sitting on the hen-house.[1]

Dodie Smith, *I Capture the Castle*

In *The Art of Thinking*, Ernest Dimnet recommends lying down in the morning, with a cup of strong coffee, and thinking.[2] This is a venue for thought many find rewarding—lying in bed or on a couch, scanning the freshest mind of the day for insight, thinking about the day ahead, or revisiting the last thoughts of the night before. Lying in bed before sleep at night can be similarly rewarding. When the surrounding rooms are silent, there comes the enticing prospect of lying comfortably, thinking uninterrupted thoughts—perhaps the only time thoughts have the promise of being uninterrupted. Unfortunately, on days when nighttime is the only time to think, it hardly needs to be said but that the would-be thinker is, by then, too tired to think. Some nights, two concurrent nights would be welcome—one in which to lie awake and think, the other in which to sleep.

Different types of thinking may be catalyzed by different surroundings. Where brainstorming may come easily, untangling a difficult problem may be impossible. Author Julia Cameron[3] admits to doing much of her idea-generating thinking while driving. To actually put those ideas on paper, however, she has several workstations in her home. Not only does moving from the room with lilac walls and lace curtains to the aqua picnic table facing the mountains provide a change of scenery and routine for long writing days, but the change of sensory stimuli contributes to her progress.

Francie held the books close and hurried home, resisting the temptation to sit on the first stoop she came to, to start reading.

Home at last and now it was the time she had been looking forward to all week: fire-escape-sitting time. She put a small rug on the fire-escape and got the pillow from her bed and propped it against the bars. Luckily there was ice in the icebox. She chipped off a small piece and put it in a glass of water. The pink-and-white peppermint wafers bought that morning were arranged in a little bowl, cracked, but of a pretty blue color. She arranged glass, bowl and book on the window sill and climbed out on the fire-escape.[4]

Betty Smith, *A Tree Grows in Brooklyn*

To review: Good places to think—at the library, in the kitchen sink, on top of the henhouse, in bed or on the couch (with coffee), in the car, in a lilac room, at an aqua picnic table, on a fire escape . . .

Solitude

I heard a piece of charm school–type advice back in my high school days: If a girl wants a certain boy to talk to her, she should not always locate herself in a group of girls. Amid the surrounding attention, the boy might be intimidated and stay away. Good advice for a sixteen-year-old. Here is good advice for an adult: If you want significant thoughts to visit you, don't always locate yourself in a group. Amid the competing voices, your own thoughts may never be realized.

Well, I went and was tinglingly alone. It was delicious . . . And I looked at the people who were not alone and I pitied them. For each person had to share his impression with someone else. And it would just be thrown away, like as not, and each person had to add, to superimpose on his impression the impression of his neighbor. Neither of them had the whole perfect fruit.[5]

Anne Morrow Lindbergh, *Hour of Gold, Hour of Lead*

Unless one is alone, one's own thoughts can't be thought. They can't move about freely without being falsely realigned according to the magnetic pull of another's thoughts. Only in solitude can one's thoughts return to a natural form, like a child's toy with built-in shape memory that returns to its original shape after being poked and prodded. Only in solitude can thoughts be followed to completion, new directions chosen, and work proceed unquestioned. Only when alone can we invariably take ourselves and our work seriously without apology or explanation.

In a group, we can gather ideas, opinions, information, and hints of things that interest, inspire, or trouble us. The things of worth, however, must be brought back with us to a time of solitude and reflection, where we can hold them next to our own thoughts and knowledge. We can then look for points of connection and opportunities for expansion and transformation—like a game of solitaire in which a deck of solitary cards is transformed into a complex integrated whole through the simple actions of linking one card with another and one accumulated batch of cards to another.

I want silence more than anything, the peace of solitude, long hours for reflection.[6]

Daphne du Maurier, *Myself When Young*

It is vital to find a way to be alone and think. While on a tour of Thomas Edison's home in Fort Myers, Florida, I heard the tour guide reveal the great inventor's scheme to achieve solitude: When the house was occupied with visitors, he often excused himself to go fishing in the backyard canal. He would sit with his fishing line in the water for hours. Unknown to the visitors, his line had no hook. It simply was his excuse to be alone and think. Who would disturb a man who was fishing?

In the midst of busy lives and many demands, we may have to be clever, like Edison, in order to find time alone to think. It is a necessity, not a luxury. And it is a universal necessity, not limited only to the introverted minority who thrive on solitude. Even extroverts, who thrive on the company of others, need solitude. After all, each of us has a life on which to reflect, a mind to develop, challenges to face, and a self to understand.

Cerebral Privacy

Inside my head is my only truly private place. Everything else—body, actions—may be seen, known, by someone sometime. Thoughts are the truest freedom. Their origin and their destination may remain unknown to family members. Their plodding course or racing gallop may be hidden from work colleagues. If they are agreeable or ornery, no one need know. Do I agree with what's being said across the room? I alone can choose to affirm yes or challenge no.

Why does this matter? Because once I realize that I truly can control the privacy of my brain, I have tremendous freedom for thoughts of all varieties and magnitude. I can build on a theory, compose a story, frame an argument, seek answers to a question—all without passing it first before critical eyes and ears. To try out a new style of dress, I must risk the reaction of the public eye. To try out a new style of thought, I can do it while sitting at a table of eight and no one is the wiser.

Unless, of course, I open my mouth.

My mouth is the loose link in the privacy fence around my brain. Once it opens and a connection is made between my mouth and the portion of my brain housing my private thought factory, those thoughts can be converted to words more quickly than my good sense can shout, "Stop!" Once spoken, thoughts are fair game for disagreement, challenge, rebuke, and so on.

Young, vulnerable thoughts may not be ready for challenge; likewise, they may not be ready for agreement. Agreement may prematurely tell my brain that its work is done on this subject, that it can now move on, when in reality, its work is far from complete.

Perhaps the revealed thought is at such an early stage that once converted into meager words it is used up and gone forever. Perhaps I disagree with something so ever present around me that my mind remains my only venue for civil disobedience. Perhaps I am surrounded by such confusion that my mind remains my link to reality.

Other opportunities of making her observations could not fail to occur. Anne had soon been in company with all the four together often enough to have an opinion, though too wise to acknowledge as much at home . . .[7]

Jane Austen, Persuasion

Maybe the thought released through my mouth is still in the incoherent, unjelled phase. "How stupid," my listener's eyes, if not mouth, would say after hearing my cognitive jumble. Feeling then incapable of anything other than a stupid idea, I would feel it best for all humankind to stop any further thought on the subject.

How much better to roll a thought around in my head for a while. Write it down. Look at it from all angles. Live with it awhile. Wait until I can hold up my thought to the inspection of others without, or in spite of, clenching self-consciousness in my gut. Then choose to open my mouth and say, "This is what I've been thinking about."

Props for Thought

Like props in a play that ground the action to time, place, and mood, tangible objects can ground our thoughts, containing them to a task at hand, a problem to be solved, a mood to be maintained, or an idea to be pondered.

Symbols are one sort of object that can act as a prop for our thoughts. Symbols are infused with meaning and prompt the viewer of the symbol to consider that meaning. The Celtic knot hanging on the chain around my neck—a symbol of eternity. The ring on my left hand—a symbol of lifelong commitment. A snake wound around a pole—a symbol of healing, reminiscent of Moses lifting up the snake on a pole in order to save his people from a devastating plague.[8] Look on the lifted-up snake, said the Lord, and you will live.

A crucifix. A cross. The agony of Christ; the victory of Christ; the depth of his love for us. The bread. The cup. Tangible concrete markers of Christ in us; Christ's body given for us.

Father Rivas reached the Canon of the Mass and the consecration of the bread. Marta was watching her man with an expression of pride. The priest lifted up the maté gourd and spoke the only phrases of the Mass which Doctor Plarr had for some reason never forgotten. "As often as you do these things you shall do them in memory of Me."[9]

Graham Greene, *The Honorary Consul*

Around my office, a visitor will find a number of symbols disguised as ordinary objects: rocks from the shores of Lake Superior (calmness, solidity), a natural sea sponge from the Gulf of Mexico (the cycle of emptying and refilling), a candle (inspiration), pictures of my family (love, relationship, joy), a Morgan Yacht Corporation mug (memories of youth), a baby picture of myself (who was I born to be?), and numerous other objects that prompt my mind to think in certain ways, about certain things.

Concentrations of words also serve as props for thought, opening up or directing them whenever they are read. A potent question visually set before you can be a powerful trigger for thought. A quote or proverb written on a note card and carried in a pocket or tacked next to the computer or kitchen sink can be instructive and inspiring, a reminder of truth, a point of focus, providing a foothold from which your mind can proceed higher.

Environmental Affairs

Not all environments are conducive to thinking. I used to work for a woman who had this to say to her staff: "Don't think. Thinking gets you in trouble." My boss was essentially saying, "Turn off your mind." Although it is uncommon to be given this message overtly, it is quite common for people and institutions to give us this very message subtly.

"Sending a girl to college is like pouring water in your shoes," he still loves to say, as often as possible. "It's hard to say which is worse, seeing it run out and waste the water, or seeing it hold in and wreck the shoes."[10]

Barbara Kingsolver, *The Poisonwood Bible*

In 1929, novelist Virginia Woolf lamented the limited access women had to the academic resources of society in her day. Her solution: Challenge women to see their minds as independent of the restrictions imposed on them. "Lock up your libraries if you like; but there is no gate, no lock, no bolt that you can set upon the freedom of my mind."[11]

Today, few official social or physical restrictions are placed on the mental development and accomplishment of women in Western society. Yet the reality of our social milieu is that beauty is often elevated over brains, action over reflection, fun over study, and busyness over contemplation.

If you examine the environment in which you work and live, and determine that it is one that encourages and affirms thought, then you are fortunate. If you determine that it does not, however, then you must think even more than you already do in order to figure a way around the barriers. You need either to seek out or to create a climate that encourages and affirms thought. Cultivate an attitude that projects vibrant mental activity as the norm. Find people in your life who share this attitude. Take advantage of available cultural resources that feed your mind.

There are days, sometimes long runs of days, during which the world places on us no immediate demand for thought, offers no incentive or reward for thought, or tries to counteract our internal drive for thought. During such days, we must beware of demanding little of our minds. We must be our own taskmasters. The demand to think and to keep thinking, to spend from our minds extravagantly, must come from within, regardless of outside demand, expectation, or affirmation.

What Is It Worth?

Madame Marie Curie was born in 1867 in Warsaw, Poland—a time and a country in which free thinking was met with suspicion, particularly if it occurred among young women. Along with her sister Bronya, she attended secret sessions of the "Floating University," which included

71

lessons in anatomy, natural history, and sociology. Those who attended this "university" risked a great deal for an opportunity to think and learn. "The disciples gathered to the number of eight or ten at a time and took notes: they passed pamphlets and articles from one to the other; at the slightest noise they trembled, for if they had been discovered by the police it would have meant prison for all of them."[12]

Marie Curie's willingness to sacrifice for an opportunity to think and learn continued into her young adult life. While attending school at the Sorbonne in Paris, she often lived on only buttered bread and tea.[13] She heated her tea over an alcohol lamp. She had only a few threadbare dresses. Her only furnishings were a table, chair, bed, and trunk. Her desire to meet her goal of learning was so great that frugality became a tool to attain that goal. Her efforts were clearly successful, as she became the first woman to receive a Nobel Prize.

What are learning and thought worth to you?

I could easily go on writing all night but I can't really see and it's extravagant on paper, so I shall merely think. Contemplation seems to be about the only luxury that costs nothing.[14]

Dodie Smith, *I Capture the Castle*

Of course, to think well at any given moment costs no more money than to think poorly. In fact, it is certainly cheaper in the long run. And as we go through life, we had just as well learn from our experiences as not. But to have time to soak in deeper thought, to practice new ways of thinking, to learn new fields often may require some expenditure of money, some degree of financial means. With so many dollars accounted for simply by living—buying food, clothing, shelter, health care—it may seem impossible to allocate funds to the "luxury" of learning and thinking.

What might you need to give up or exchange in order to expand and enrich your thought life? Is the cost of an adult education class at your local university too high? A book budget? Some periodicals? A retreat? Would you consider a sabbatical leave from work to pursue long-term focused study? A trip to somewhere new and invigorating? A place of solitude? A desk to call your own? A library card and an afternoon to yourself?

The acquisition of this room was the beginning of a new era in Thea's life. It was one of the most important things that ever happened to her . . . her mind worked better. She thought things out more clearly. Pleasant plans and ideas occurred to her which had never come before.[5]

Willa Cather, *The Song of the Lark*

To Everything a Season

I watched my friend walk into the room, carrying her newborn baby. She doesn't care to think about much else right now other than her baby. There is not much else she *can* think about right now. Just a few weeks earlier, she was sitting at her desk in her office, applying her mind to her employer's assignments. At home, she was balancing the checkbook, reading novels and parenting guides, decorating a nursery. Today, and for a long time to come, her mind will be almost fully on her baby.

I remember those days of early motherhood when every ounce of my mental and physical energy was held in reserve for and spent on my young children. I also remember a particular moment when I felt the intensity of my focus lift ever so slightly. At that particular moment, after a long stretch—several years maybe—of reading only children's books aloud to my children or books related to raising children, it occurred to me that I might get a book from the library completely unrelated to children or parenting. I might get a book for my own personal interest and pleasure. And I did. If checking a book out of the library could be called exhilarating, that moment certainly was.

There is a time for everything.[16]

From the Book of Ecclesiastes

Some seasons of life require our mental energy to contract tightly around one object: a baby, a child, a sick family member, school, a new job. And to give that object our finest mental energy can be some of the most important and fulfilling work we will ever do. But these objects don't hold us forever—children are not always small and helpless; jobs don't remain new. Seasons change and our mental energy can, and must, expand and shift.

Typically, the further we move from the years of establishing family or career, the more freedom we have in choosing the objects on which we focus our mental energy. The ability to do this—to respond to the changing seasons of life with appropriate refocusing of mental energy—has tremendous significance in terms of what we continue to accomplish throughout the duration of our lives as well as our sense of well-being. Mental energy without a focus leaves us restless until it is redirected. The mind idles high, waiting for the opportunity to accelerate, for the road ahead to open. Mental energy that continues for an extended time without a focus or an opportunity for release is in danger of eventually dissipating.

Can my friend with the newborn baby imagine the huge reservoir of mental energy that she will have available to reclaim as her child moves from infant to toddler to child to teen to man? Probably not. Nor would she wish to imagine this, so complete is her loving focus now. Yet women ten, fifteen, or twenty years down the road from her can certainly predict the need that she will someday surely feel for something else toward which to direct her mental energy.

At forty I am beginning to learn the mechanism of my own brain—how to get the greatest amount of pleasure and work out of it.[7]

Virginia Woolf, *A Writer's Diary*

6

MENTAL READINESS

Steel before Paint

When building a house, steel comes before paint, concrete before tile, and wood before curtains. A certain order of construction must be followed. Before a picture can be selected and hung on a nail hammered through a wallpapered wall; before a window can be hung with sash and hardware and covered with a window treatment of pleat or flounce; before paint is brushed or tile is laid or quarter-rounds are mitered, the structure that will receive all of the above must stand strong and stable.

Steel. Concrete. Wood. These materials of strength and stability must first be selected and placed with care and precision to form the foundational structure, or scaffold, of a building. This scaffold is the bare minimum a structure needs in order to exist, in order to begin to become what it will be.

The mind one uses and adds to all the days of one's life is not unlike a building. It has the potential of being as functional as any house, as fine as any cathedral, and as soaring as any skyscraper. But to build it functional and fine and soaring, one must first put in place a supporting framework. Without this mental architecture, one's mind is at risk of accumulating a mass of random thoughts, facts, questions, and ideas, and then getting buried under the sheer weight and volume of it all.

And what is the supporting framework of a mind? Just as the scaffold of a building must relate to and serve the form and function of the building's raison d'être, so the scaffold of a mind must relate to and serve the form and function of a person's reason for being. And so almost by definition, the mind's scaffold needs a spiritual construction. Beams of truth to hold the weight of everything else.

The steel beams of truth of the Christian faith are described in the Apostle's Creed: God is triune, comprising God the Father, God the Son, and God the Holy Spirit. God the Father Almighty created the heavens and earth. Jesus Christ is God's son, our Savior. He was born of the Virgin Mary, suffered and was crucified, and returned to life the third day. He ascended into heaven and sits with God where he will be the future judge of all who have lived. In Christ sins are forgiven, the dead are resurrected, and life is everlasting.

This sparse, but substantive, scaffolding stands with enormous strength, ready to be filled in and added to throughout a life shaped by other interests, calls, joys, and needs. Additional scaffolding representing the core elements of parenting, nursing, accounting, marathon running, corporate law, caregiving, and so on, can likewise be erected and filled in and added to as needed.

With such mental architecture in place, a natural order develops within the mind that can absorb the weight and volume of daily thoughts, facts, questions, and ideas. Just as a good outline, when one writes a paper, can organize thoughts making each one subservient within, rather than competitive with, a hierarchy of main points.

"How long will it be before the book's finished?"

"Finished? It isn't even begun! I'm still collecting material—though that'll go on indefinitely, of course." He began to walk about, talking more to himself than to me. "I believe I could make a start now if I could get a scaffolding that really satisfied me. I need a backbone."[1]

Dodie Smith, *I Capture the Castle*

Ingredients in Advance

Maybe it is a rejection of the rote memory practiced throughout school, but I find it easy to justify not memorizing much of anything anymore. After all, no matter what information I may need, I'm sure I can find it when I need it. There's little reason to memorize or internalize it in the form of knowledge in advance, as I can always refer elsewhere for it.

But there is a flaw in this mind-set: Before I can put the needed information to use, I must take the time and expend the energy to ferret it out. Next, I must rethink it and blow the dust off the corollary thoughts and information I once associated with it. It is not surprising, therefore, that when faced with finding information that I have chosen not to commit to memory, I may choose not to bother. I may not even bother with the project to which I wanted to apply the information. It is not surprising that I let the thing I wanted to do go undone.

In contrast, keeping key information in my working memory changes everything. Knowing the information ahead of time—before starting a project—sets all ingredients in place in advance, ready to be added to my mental alchemy pot exactly as each is needed. It's the difference between starting a recipe and then having to make a separate trip to the store for each ingredient versus starting with all the ingredients on hand.

John Locke said this about memory:

> . . . he who, through this default in his memory, has not the ideas that are really preserved there, ready at hand when need and occasion calls for them, were almost as good be without them quite, since they serve him to little purpose. The dull man, who loses an opportunity, whilst he is seeking in his mind for those ideas that should serve his turn, is not much more happy in his knowledge than one that is perfectly ignorant. It is the business therefore of the memory to furnish to the mind those dormant ideas which it has present occasion for; in the having them ready at hand on all occasions, consists that which we call invention, fancy, and quickness of parts.[2]

If you think you don't have time to learn something that you will soon need to use, you may be wrong. You may not have time not to learn it. With a loaded working memory, you can instantaneously combine pieces of known information, immediately add new knowledge to the scaffold of what you already know.

A note of caution: Time is not saved and improvement to a project is not made if you aren't selective about the information you commit to working memory. Too much information, too many facts randomly in your brain become overwhelming, obscuring the scaffold beams with material that is decorative or superfluous. So before busily and earnestly logging facts into your working memory, you may want to acquire a broad overview of the project or topic in order to determine the main, or scaffold, points. What is foundational? Establish that first—you can't build on a foundation you haven't yet incorporated into your working thoughts.

This combination of foundational scaffold and essential information in working memory accomplishes two things: It allows ideas and efforts to be fruitful and not wasted, and it stills a mind busy with disconnected pieces of information.

Great Expectations

Each morning that you are privileged to awaken, no matter how ordinary your life, expect your mind to be wooed—by the beauty of nature, the voice of a friend, the words of a poet, the moving of God's Spirit. Expect it to be wooed to go higher, deeper, broader.

Wake every morning sensitive to the wooing, to the still small voice calling to your brain to do any of the numerous things of which it is capable. Brush your teeth while telling yourself that you'll gain more understanding during the coming day, that you'll end the day with greater depth and breadth than when you started. Drink your coffee with gratitude that mental dullness and boredom are the exception rather than the rule for a mind in love with

God. Expect that your attitude of expectancy will not go disappointed.

"Since the first day that you set your mind to gain understanding and to humble yourself before your God, your words were heard, and I have come in response to them."[3]

From the Book of Daniel

Just as it's possible to sleep through a morning wake-up alarm when you know it's only for the person sleeping next to you, so it's possible to miss a mental wake-up alarm if you aren't anticipating it. Put your mind in a mode that is alert to mental markers—words, signs, experiences—that trigger thought. The markers might be related to your areas of interest, current questions or projects, or ongoing joys or challenges. Or they might represent a totally new direction your life is about to take.

Consider the list below and imagine how life might be different if each of the items listed were greeted with an active and confident expectation that something remarkable could develop as a result. Imagine what God could do with the events of your life—whether extraordinary or ordinary—if you meet such ideas not only with an open heart toward God but with a willing and expectant mind.

A lost job	An unanswered prayer
A sudden new and powerful thought	An answered prayer
	A "coincidence"
A new assignment or job	A dilemma
A new friend	An awakening of curiosity
A challenge	A glimmer of delight
A discomfort	A mistake
A difficult person	Success
Sudden joy	Words that "jump off a
A thought of "Wow"	page"

Words that keep ringing in your head	Beauty
	A perplexing question
Something common but newly noticed	A mystery
	A choice

Like Pavlov, who trained his dog to salivate at the sound of the dinner bell by building an association between the bell and the dinner, train your mind to "drool" with anticipation of the food for thought and mental growth that can result from any of these mental triggers. Watch for things to wonder about. Look for things to figure out. Know that wonderful, fruitful experiences are coming your way.

IT'S JUST WHAT OLE GOLLY SAYS . . . SHE SAYS WHEN PEOPLE DON'T DO ANYTHING THEY DON'T THINK ANYTHING, AND WHEN THEY DON'T THINK ANYTHING THERE'S NOTHING TO THINK ABOUT THEM. IF I HAD A DUMBWAITER I WOULD LOOK IN IT ALL THE TIME TO SEE IF ANYBODY WAS IN IT.[4]

Louise Fitzhugh, *Harriet the Spy*

Captured on Paper

We all have them. Cotton candy thoughts that quickly dissolve, despite our best efforts to savor them. Even though we may have no trouble remembering our neighbor's phone number or the preamble of the Constitution, we can't necessarily remember a great thought that dawned just before buttering the bread that is now being swallowed. In *Bird by Bird*, writer Anne Lamott shares this lament: "That is one of the worst feelings I can think of, to have had a wonderful moment or insight or vision or phrase, to know you had it, and then to lose it."[5]

Those of us afflicted with the habitual loss of great thoughts need to find a way to stop such loss. And the most effective way seems to be to capture thoughts on paper as soon as possible, even at the moment of appearance. A significant insight or moment that is not written down is like a gift received and opened but forgotten on the seat of a disappearing train.

Anne Lamott's solution is the common index card. In her essay entitled "Index Cards," she describes her habit of never leaving home without a pen and at least one index card in her back pocket, folded lengthwise, of course, to avoid adding unnecessary bulk.[6] Kinsey Millhone, protagonist sleuth of Sue Grafton's best-selling alphabet mystery series, also is a fan of the index card approach. Millhone's dramatic investigations of murders and other crimes are frequently punctuated with stops to buy index cards or to throw a fresh pack of them in her purse.

An index card isn't the solution of choice for everyone. Some have success with the note-on-the-back-of-the-hand approach, reminiscent of junior high. A purse- or pocket-size spiral notebook. A sketch pad. A small tape recorder. If you don't already have the practice of recording your thoughts, choose something, carry it regularly, and start to bank your valuable mental currency. A quick written word or phrase that will open up in your mind when reread is sufficient. The details can be filled in later. The note may be transferred to a journal or file, or to a simple growing pile where you know you'll be able to retrieve a variety of stockpiled thoughts.

I used to imagine I could hold it all in my head, but memory has a way of pruning and deleting, eliminating anything that doesn't seem relevant at the moment. Later, it's the odd unrelated detail that sometimes makes the puzzle parts rearrange themselves like magic. The very act of taking pen to paper somehow gooses the brain into making the leap. It doesn't always happen in the moment, but without the concrete notation, the data disappear.[7]

Sue Grafton, *"O" Is for Outlaw*

Your memory is assisted by more than the physical note you have made. The very act of writing, of moving hand and pen across paper puts other parts of you in cooperation with your memory. Your hands have now participated in your thought. Your eyes have seen it written on a piece of paper. The visual picture of the color of ink, the space it takes up on the page, the look of the index card or notebook, the side of the page in the notebook, the size of the scribble, a circle or bracket placed around it—all help lodge it in your mind.

Ernest Dimnet wrote, "The moment we realize that any thought, ours or borrowed, is pregnant enough not to be wasted, or original enough not to be likely to come back again, we must fix it on paper."[8] Like straw awaiting its transformation to gold, recorded insights, memories, and other thoughts are raw material waiting to be pondered and transformed.

Into Words

The assignment: To communicate to you something that is inside of me. To do this, I could draw or paint a picture, perform a dance, use body language, or compose a melody. Or I can choose words. Words that when strung together slide thoughts from my mind into yours as easily as pearls along an unknotted string.

Language is to the mind more than light is to the eye.[9]
William Gibson, *The Miracle Worker*

Most of us, most of the time, rely on words for communication. And for most of us, most of the time, the words at the forefront of our minds are appropriate choices with which to pass on our thoughts, and their selection is therefore not a problem. At other times, however, selecting just the right word can be as difficult as selecting just the right bathing suit.

As the importance or complexity of the thought increases, so does the difficulty of choosing the right word and the consequence of choosing the wrong word. The subtlety of thought, the barely discernible difference between the way I see something and the way you may see something, can be made known only if I choose just the right word with the same barely discernible difference from the one you would choose. If I choose the wrong word—one with unintended or ambiguous meaning—I deliver the wrong message.

In turn, the listener also bears responsibility for words and their meaning. What I hear someone saying to me is a function not just of how precisely she has chosen her words, but of how precisely I define those words as I hear them. Shades of meaning can vary considerably between speaker and hearer if they don't take equal care with their words.

85

The benefit of choosing just the right word is not only that it helps the other person understand what I am thinking, but also that it helps me clarify what I'm thinking. Choosing precise words sharpens my thinking, because when two words are before me with slightly different meanings, I must choose: Do I mean this or that? Thinking about the difference between word meanings can also open up new ideas and new ways of looking at something. For example, consider the subtle difference in meaning between "you accomplished" versus "you achieved" or "I love" versus "I adore."

To say the very thing you really mean, the whole of it, nothing more or less than what you really mean; that's the whole art and joy of words.[10]

C. S. Lewis, *Till We Have Faces*

I have a worn hardcover copy of *Webster's New Dictionary of Synonyms: A Dictionary of Discriminated Synonyms with Antonyms and Analogous and Contrasted Words*. I bought it used, with slightly yellowed pages and a persistent cigarette smell. I use it nearly daily. It differs from a thesaurus in that it offers more than a list of apparently equivalent words that may be substituted one for the other. It offers explanations of word choices, providing "the means of making clear comparisons between words of a common denotation and to enable [readers] to distinguish the differences in implications, connotations, and applications among such words and to choose for their purposes the precisely suitable words."[11]

As artful as any strokes and steps and notes of those who paint or dance or write music, precisely chosen words allow you to tell someone else what is inside of you. Maybe more importantly, they allow you to think more clearly about what is inside of yourself.

A Daily Prism

"God be in my head and in my understanding,"[12] sing the Chamber Singers from my sons' high school on the compact disc that swirls in its player. These same words should be the words that swirl in my mind and lift off my lips every morning. God present in my head like a prism, transforming slurry into focused color and beauty.

This is a transformation I need. Daily. Let me suggest three reasons why.

Reason 1. I need divine order. On any given morning, my mind doesn't take long to fill. As nighttime dreams dissipate, the issues of the day stream in like water running to fill a void. The day can then start to gallop away in a direction I hadn't intended, toward a destination unknown, with me unprepared and in a mood I dislike. Only to be suddenly whirled around by a whistle from a different direction. Priorities somersault over each other. Like a faulty rein, my mind is fastened to the galloping day, but is ineffective in directing it. I need order that can only be attained by placing God first and foremost.

Seek first his kingdom and his righteousness.[13]

From the Book of Matthew

Reason 2. I need to be reminded. Reminded that the way I look at the world isn't necessarily the same as do the hosts of the *Today Show* or the columnists in the op-ed page of the morning paper or the contributors to the e-mail newsgroup to which I subscribe. Reminded of life according to Christian doctrine and of the scaffold of Christian faith on which my mind must be daily centered. Reminded that the joy in my life is a gift from God, and the pain in my life is not suffered alone. Reminded that I live accountable to God. Reminded that I am loved by the Creator of the universe and was designed for more than success. Reminded that my soul is my most important possession. Reminded that Christ's peace is mine.

Reason 3. I need help thinking. As the Creator of the universe and all that is therein, and as the Creator of me and all that is therein, God simply must be in my head to help me think as well as I can throughout my day and to give me insight into things true and wonderful, or deep and awesome, or painful and confusing as only the Creator of me and the universe can provide.

Yes, God simply must be in my head and understanding. He should not be left off to the side trying to peek inside, or overlaid, buried, and pressed out by what might be center stage in my head when left to my own devices. He must be exactly in the center of the hustle and bustle of neuron activity, where days are shaped, intentions set, directions planned, and insights discerned.

Inviting God to be in one's head and one's understanding at the beginning of and throughout the day allows him, his words, and his ways to be as panes in a stained glass window filtering light across the day. Prayer, Scripture, devotional reading, music, morning Mass, meditation—all are ways to extend the invitation.

The morning sun burned through the stained-glass windows, melting their fulgent colors and splashing them across the congregation, like jewels tossed down to the faithful.[14]

Faith Sullivan, *The Empress of One*

A Preference for Knowledge

I went to the library seeking books on a subject that interested me and about which I had been reading. My search was successful, and so I proceeded to the checkout counter with several books in hand. But before I could reach the counter, an unmistakable "No" reverberated in my mind. I didn't need one more written word on this subject. And maybe not on any subject for a while.

Let me explain: The corridor on my side of the bed houses an assortment of stacks. Mostly there are books: books I've read, books I haven't read; books from the public library, books from my personal library, books on loan from friends; old books that I'd like to revisit, new books still in the shopping bag because I feel too guilty having spent the money to take them out. At odd intervals between books lie index cards bearing ideas or to-do lists, scraps revealing a reminder about something, or correspondence awaiting a response. There are also magazines, which I find I seldom read while they are current. I have similar stacks in my office and on assorted table surfaces.

In spite of this abundance of words on bound and unbound papers, on table surfaces and in floor stacks, I have a tendency to want more. Yet that day at the library, when I just said no, I knew I had reached my saturation point for information. Why did I need more?

What was I waiting for?

Gathering information can be fun to do and gratifying to have done. And it is necessary. Yet it can be like hoarding food: All the unused goodness starts to spoil and ultimately serves no purpose. It is also not unlike materialism, but instead of filling our homes with too much furniture or our closets with too many clothes, it fills us with too many facts, words, and data.

Facts point in all directions, it seems to me, like the thousands of twigs on a tree. It's only the life of the tree that has unity and goes up — only the green blood that springs, like a fountain, at the stars.[5]

G. K. Chesterton, "The Tremendous Adventure of Major Brown"

If we become satisfied with information in abundance, we may not take the next step, the step for which the information has been provided—converting the information to knowledge. For the practical purpose of this book, I'll distinguish between these terms by contrasting them: *Information* is to gathering as *knowledge* is to integrating; information is to borrowing as knowledge is to possessing; information is to lying on the surface as knowledge is to sinking in deep. To create a culinary picture: Information is like individual small bowls, each filled with olives, peppers, provolone cheese, salami, or olive oil dressing. In contrast, knowledge is like those same ingredients all placed into one large bowl, tossed gently, and allowed to marinate until the flavors are married and a complete antipasto salad is ready to be enjoyed.

The joy of information is not in its collection, but in its transformation to knowledge, in blending together discrete units of information into ideas, concepts, understanding, mastery.

---7---

BEFOGGED

Clarity

Images of clarity are pleasing. Clarity suggests trustworthiness, safety, beauty, and worth.

Clear water, clear diamond, clear blue sky.

Clear mind.

The mind houses many important processes: awareness, imagination, intuition, learning, memory, problem solving, perception, creativity, judgment, decision making. It is reasonable to assume that each of these processes goes much better when one's mind is clear instead of cloudy.

*"I'm extremely sleepy," he said apologetically, but firmly.
"After all, it's been rather a tiring day, and—as someone
said—I will meet my God with an unclouded mind."[1]*

Charles Williams, *War in Heaven*

Consider lack of sleep, a common cause of a clouded
mind. Sleep deprivation is associated with a decline in creative thinking processes, more errors on tasks that require
ongoing vigilance, poorer performance and mood, and an
increase in motor vehicle accidents.

In addition to lack of sleep, other factors can create a
clouded mind. Too much sleep, too little exercise, boredom, and prolonged mental lulling can produce a groggy,
drugged effect. Too much sugar or caffeine, or too little
protein can make concentration difficult, and a growing
list of nutrients are believed to be part of optimal brain
health. The effect of alcohol can be anything from a decreased definition and focus of thoughts to an absence of
intentional or directed thought. And stress and emotion
can take away mental clarity as easily as a spoonful of
drink-mix powder can cloud a glass of water.

The goal for a thinking woman is to observe, imagine,
intuit, learn, perceive, remember, solve, perceive, create,
judge, and decide as finely as her abilities allow. For these,
one needs a clear mind.

Melancholy

The term *melancholy* describes a mood that many, if not
all of us, find ourselves in from time to time. It suggests a
time of being a bit down, a bit sad, deep in thought, quiet
and solitary.

According to *Webster's New Dictionary of Synonyms,* the word *melancholy* stresses "a quality that inspires pensiveness or sad reflection or awakens mournful thoughts or recollections which are not only not necessarily painful or disagreeable, but often agreeable, especially to the poetic or thoughtful mind."[2]

Without any scientific proof, I believe that a limited amount of melancholy is a good thing. Sober introspection is almost forced upon us, along with all its benefits, such as soul searching, self-realization, insight, confession, prayer, meditation, and decision.

Melancholy, however, presents a risk for mental clouding when it becomes unchecked. A prolonged and steady dose of pensive reflection can become hard to break free of. The wave of slight sadness and need for solitude that triggered the melancholy and gained its benefits can continue to break over us, causing us to lose sight of the coexisting reality of joy, peace, and companionship. A clear mind becomes cloudy.

It never occurred to her that if the drainpipes of a house are clogged, the rain may collect in pools on the roof; and she suspected no danger until suddenly she discovered a crack in the wall.[3]

Gustave Flaubert, *Madame Bovary*

Much of the Book of Psalms gives voice to a persistent melancholy, often on the edge of despair. Consider these words as an example:

> My soul refused to be comforted.
> I remembered you, O God, and I groaned;
> I mused, and my spirit grew faint . . .
> I was too troubled to speak.[4]

The grayness of unchecked melancholy comes down over the head, wraps itself around the shoulders, weighs upon the chest, sits inside the gut.

How to break free? How to stop the wave?

Read what the psalmist decides to do:

> I will remember the deeds of the LORD;
>   yes, I will remember your miracles of long ago.
> I will meditate on all your works
>   and consider all your mighty deeds.[5]

The psalmist suggests that an "I will" directive brings the needed limit to melancholy. Like a foghorn through the gray murk that calls one's mind to attention, that gives direction to the way out. And the way out lies in the words that follow the "I will": "remember the deeds of the LORD . . . remember your miracles of long ago . . . meditate on all your works . . . consider all your mighty deeds."

A legitimate question, however, is how can a person summon the wherewithal to consider the wonders and deeds of the Lord when in a clouded-mind state of unchecked melancholy?

One suggestion is to use the ancient words already written in the Book of Lamentations for this very purpose. Write the words on an index card and keep it in your pocket or purse. Or store the words in your memory. Claim the "I will" directive and read or recite these words of God's love, hope, compassion, and faithfulness:

> My soul is downcast within me.
> Yet this I call to mind
>   and therefore I have hope:
> Because of the LORD's great love we are not consumed,
>   for his compassions never fail.
> They are new every morning;
>   great is your faithfulness . . .

The LORD is good to those whose hope is in him,
  to the one who seeks him;
it is good to wait quietly
  for the salvation of the LORD. [6]

Alternatively, choose any of a number of verses from the Psalms. Or make another card containing the words of Christ from the Book of John: "Peace I leave with you; my peace I give you . . . Do not let your hearts be troubled"[7] Or go to your journal in which you have recorded the wonders and deeds of the Lord as they have appeared in your life.

For he dreamed of peace by day and night . . . Peace seemed to him the most beautiful word in the language: My peace I give you, my peace I leave with you: O Lamb of God, who takest away the sins of the world, grant us thy peace. In the Mass he pressed his fingers against his eyes to keep the tears of longing in. [8]

Graham Greene, *The Heart of the Matter*

Is there any good reason not to remember, meditate on, and consider the wonders and works of the Lord? Why not remind yourself in some simple ways of joy beyond the present mood? Why not lift the cloud?

Boredom

An uneasy feeling had been gathering for days before I realized that I was bored. And I wasn't sure why. Was it from days of doing less than I usually do? Was it a drop in adrenaline? Was it the heat? The humidity? Too much sleep? Not enough fun?

Early boredom is a potentially dangerous state. What starts out as innocent boredom can become chronic, deteriorating into melancholy, rudeness, disengagement, and perhaps most serious of all, overeating. Chronic boredom replaces vibrancy with dullness. The mind gets used to this state of reduced energy and loses, at least temporarily, its expectation of full life.

> *"Seems rather foolish to be unpleasant, Abe . . . I can't see why you've given up about everything."*
>
> *Abe considered, trying hard not to cough or blow his nose.*
>
> *"I suppose I got bored; and then it was such a long way to go back in order to get anywhere."*[9]
>
> F. Scott Fitzgerald, *Tender Is the Night*

I'm not referring to the type of boredom to which the mind is lulled by a monotone speaker showing slides with lots of text in a darkened conference room after lunch. Even the most typically unbored person can't help but feel the cylinder of boredom moving over the mind, preventing that which is outside from connecting to that which is inside.

Boredom moves from this understandable and temporary reaction to a state of mind-cloud when that cylinder is allowed to remain over the mind, keeping light and stimuli out. In that state, what the outside has to offer a mind seems either worthless or beyond reach. Likewise, what a person has to give from inside seems dull and not worth the effort to put forth. In a state of chronic boredom, the mind's contents are not in their usual state of being present, available, and wanting release; rather, they are locked away. It's as if the mind sees the visiting boredom approaching, recognizes that it won't be used for a while, and so takes a break, locking the door behind itself.

> *My parish is bored stiff; no other word for it. Like so many others! We can see them being eaten up by boredom, and we can't do anything about it. Someday perhaps we shall catch it ourselves—become aware of the cancerous growth within us. You can keep going a long time with that in you.*[10]
>
> Georges Bernanos, *Diary of a Country Priest*

Once boredom has settled in, we can't hope to be rescued by just any large whack of mental stimulation. It seems the key required to unlock boredom needs to fit one's mind uniquely, just like the pairing of a key and lock. It must be something that uniquely calls a person into the present moment and says, "Look now, this is something you don't want to miss." It might be a fascinating discourse on insects in Bolivia. It might be working in a soup kitchen. It might be an evening drive under a full moon and starry sky. It might be laughter.

Pay attention to keys that unlock your boredom. As needed, place one in the lock and turn it through an effort of will. Don't let the cylinder remain.

Emotion

> *Old Dudley felt his throat knotting up . . . His throat was drawn taut. He laid his head back and tried to clear his*

mind. There wasn't much he could think of to think about
that didn't do his throat that way."

Flannery O'Connor, "The Geranium"

It seems impossible for productive and clear thought to coexist with a throat "drawn taut," a pounding heart, or a stomach of butterflies. The overwhelming effect of strong emotion easily swirls up into even the clearest of minds. And when it does, it's as though we have no choice but to quickly excuse the mind from duty so that the emotion can inhabit it. Sometimes even a sudden reminder of an emotional time can knock us off our feet mentally. Mental energy currently occupied must quickly fly back to provide a balm for and massage past hurts.

Whether Aunt Patience took it in or not she could not tell;
certainly she nodded from time to time, and pursed her lips,
and shook her head . . . but it seemed to Mary that years of
fear and anxiety had taken away her powers of concentration,
and that some underlying terror prevented her from giving
her whole interest to any conversation.[12]

Daphne du Maurier, *Jamaica Inn*

The challenge is to bring our minds quickly back to duty. Not of course that we always want to squelch emotion and function with only thought, any more than we want to function with no thought and only emotion. But the fact of the matter is that strong emotion has the power to effectively cancel out thought. It rarely is the other way around. Strong emotion therefore becomes a risk to a clear mind. This presents a problem, because a clear mind certainly needs to be dependably involved in whatever the episode of strong emotion—be it an episode of fear, love, worry, or anger. After all, do you want to face fear with only the counsel of your emotion? Love without the confirmation of your mind? Worry without remembering prayer and promises of provision? Anger without a way to think it through?

I will keep the law given by God; sanctioned by man. I will hold to the principles received by me when I was sane, and not mad—as I am now. Laws and principles are not for the times when there is no temptation: they are for such moments as this, when body and soul rise in mutiny against their rigour . . . They have a worth—so I have always believed; and if I cannot believe it now, it is because I am insane—quite insane: with my veins running fire, and my heart beating faster than I can count its throbs. Preconceived opinions, foregone determinations, are all I have at this hour to stand by: there I plant my foot.[3]

Charlotte Brontë, *Jane Eyre*

With the help of the will, clear and productive thought can break through the cloud of strong emotion. In fact, often a powerful emotional experience is precisely the turning point for a new deeper way of thinking. But first, will and emotion have to meet, and will must supervise emotion, telling it to step to one side and allow thought to return alongside of it. As thought returns, so does all that is within a person—all one has learned, lived, believed, trusted, conquered, suffered, and loved—that is at least as strong as this temporary flare of emotion.

Thought informs emotion; emotion informs thought. In a clear mind.

Barrenness

"It will suck your mind dry," said the television advertisement for an upcoming movie. I made a mental note then and there not to see this movie. I suspect most readers of this book would have done the same thing. I also suspect that most of us don't intentionally participate in anything that over a two-hour time period could actually suck a mind dry. On the other hand, less overt forces may be accomplishing mental dehydration sip by subtle sip.

Who among us doesn't know the dead-in-the-head feeling that is the reward for watching two straight hours of sitcoms or that comes after several days in bed recovering from an illness during which all you did was stare at the ceiling or flip through fashion magazines? If this is repeated often enough, the barren brain has a hard time reviving.

In contrast to the mind-drying thoughts that remove activity from the brain, junk thoughts add activity to the brain, but not the type of life-giving activity we desire our brains to have. Junk thoughts are like e-mail viruses having a go at the cerebral hard drive. They multiply in an out-of-control fashion, attach themselves to good and worthy data stored there, and corrupt the system. They come at us from television shows, movie previews, magazine headlines, noxious people. They steal time, mental resources, and energy. They make us covetous, tempted, and insecure. It's hard to think well while being ambushed by an attack of junk.

Depletion of lively mental energy can be the result of simply being in the wrong place at the wrong time. For example, in front of the television set for too long of a time, or in a movie theater watching a particular preview instead of standing in the popcorn line, or in front of a magazine rack long enough to get pulled into buying an issue with provocative headlines, or in front of a person whose mouth, at that moment, is saying things that would better go unheard.

Choose what gives life to the mind rather than what depletes its energy.

I do not like these generalities. Soon you will be writing little books called "Deep Thoughts for the Layman," so simplified that they are positively guaranteed not to cause thinking.[4]

F. Scott Fitzgerald, *Tender Is the Night*

8

SELF-KNOWLEDGE

I Am

A teacher of an adult education class I took asked all of us to introduce ourselves by saying the following: "I am *(give your name)*, and in my hometown of *(name your hometown)*, my mom or dad *(tell one thing your mom or dad did)*." Most of the class followed the instructions, correctly and succinctly filling in the blanks as they introduced themselves. But some did not. They told their names, maiden names, parents' names, children's names. They described their homes, childhood and present, and listed their own and their parents' hometowns. They provided occupation and employment history. Some even mapped out the progression of their cities of residence, telling how they came to be in the location where they are today.

My amateur sociologic speculation was that those who broke the rules had nowhere else to share their identity. Maybe it was the first time in recent memory that someone had asked a question resembling, "Who are you?"—and the "I am" just gushed out.

I remembered how much that friendship had meant to me, that way you could just open your mouth . . . and let your whole self out, all those small mosaic pieces of self that felt barely held together with plaster of personality half the time.[1]

Anna Quindlen, *Black and Blue*

Most of us are eager to complete the sentence that starts, "I am . . ." But to accurately describe the unique person one is, beyond mere demographic data, requires a degree of self-knowledge that few of us have. In *Self-Renewal*, John Gardner writes, "By middle life most of us are accomplished fugitives from ourselves."[2]

A number of routes can be taken on the journey of self-knowledge. Some routes skirt the shoreline; others lead us deep into the core of the country.

In the 1980s, a revolution in style caused women to define their outward selves in terms of a "season" and to purge their closets of colors that were not in the same palette as their season. Women who were "autumns" no longer had use for pastel blues or pinks, and those who were "summers" avoided jewel tones.

Another chromatologic approach to self-knowledge was implied by the title of a talk I saw advertised some years ago in a Chicago newspaper, "What Color Is Your Brain?" Although I didn't hear this talk, the title implied that the audience would be asked to consider such questions as, How do I learn? What energized my mind? Interesting questions to take home from a luncheon.

Deeper and deeper one can go. The Myers-Briggs Type Indicator helps test takers understand themselves better within the context of opposite preferences on four scales. In *Introduction to Type*, Isabel Briggs Myers explains the questions posed by these four scales: Where do I prefer to place my energy, and likewise, by what am I energized—the outside world or my own inner world? How do I find out things—through my senses or my intuition? How do I make decisions—by thinking or by feeling? How do I deal with the outside world—in a planned and orderly way or in a flexible, spontaneous way?[3]

Systematic journaling allows one to travel still more deeply. Author Joanna Field began a seven-year process to discover more about herself, a quest triggered by the feeling that her life was not as it ought to be. She began to keep a diary, recording and reflecting on the experiences of each day that made her happy. From this she tried to discover who she truly was and what she really wanted out of life. She documented her experience in *A Life of One's Own*, in which she wrote, "It . . . seems to be true that one can assume and strive after a false attitude, that is, an attitude contrary to the trend of one's nature; so there may perhaps be some who, if tempted to try the same experiment, may discover as I did myself that they are quite different creatures from what they had imagined."[4]

We can also discover ourselves in the context of personal history, our individual mission, and other relationships. The preamble to an organization's constitution typically sets forth its reason for being and its history. A valid route on the journey of self-knowledge is to think through and write down your personal preamble. Where did you begin?

What is your history? What makes you unique? What is your passion and mission?

Certainly the most important question any of us can ask is: Who am I in the eyes of God? Could you give a brief autobiographical sketch of yourself to the only one who truly knows you—that is, God—to which he would reply, "Yes, that's exactly right!"?

> *It seems we need someone to know us as we are . . . But it's so much to ask of other people! Too much. Daniel makes it easier on those around him: God is the one he asks to know him as he is, to see him whole and love him still.*[5]
>
> Sue Miller, *While I Was Gone*

A Student of One's Life

Anne Morrow Lindbergh wrote, "God, let me be *conscious* of it! Let me be *conscious* of *what* is happening *while* it is happening. Let me realize it and feel it vividly. Let not the consciousness of the event (as happens so often) come to me tardily, so that I miss half the experience. Let me be *conscious* of it!"[6]

I went to hear a young woman speak who exemplified Lindbergh's attitude. This woman had walked—by herself—across the United States and had documented her experiences in a series of magazine articles. Before the program began, I met her by chance in the bathroom as we washed our hands in side-by-side sinks.

"I admire you," I said, "for doing what you did."

"But I'm no different from you," she replied with a warm smile. "Every day you get up, put on your shoes, and walk through your day doing what you need to do, right?"

No different from me? I appreciated her humble and gracious comment, yet I could think of a number of ways in which she and what she did was different from me and what I do.

The vast difference in our capacities for physical endurance notwithstanding, here is one key difference between us: She paid attention to her days of putting on her shoes and walking. She wrung all that she could out of those days as she watched for opportunity, saturated herself in experience, thought about meaning, and wrote it all down.

Instead of going through a day in the way we sometimes drive to work or the grocery store (on autopilot), what if we really paid attention to landmarks, events, sensations, and experiences along the way, as well as the feelings generated, thoughts triggered, and memories evoked? And what if at the end of the day, we listed the things we had experienced and expanded on each with a sentence or two, taking care to mention how something felt, tasted, sounded, looked, or smelled? Imagine the evidence of a rich life we would have by the end of a week.

But so many of the things on this list might appear to be such small things. Why bother to pay attention to things so small?

How long it takes to realize in one's life the intricate patterns of which everything—even a picture postcard—can form a part, and the rashness of dismissing anything as unimportant.[7]

Graham Greene, *Our Man in Havana*

Consider the Human Genome Project.[8] While the literal objects of study in this project are small, the ultimate focus is huge. This project has catalogued about 2.9 billion smaller-than-microscopic molecular bases, which when paired and grouped form 35,000 to 45,000 genes, which are organized into forty-six human chromosomes. Base pair by base pair, the investigators mapped human DNA, as part of a gene, as part of a chromosome, as part of the whole human genome, and finally as part of the key to understanding the cause and cure of human disease.

In life, as in the human genome, the little things are what the big things are made of. A pageant of discrete happenings, ideas, conversations, facts, images. Considered individually they enrich one's experience; considered together they create a life. Pay attention.

A Penny for My Thoughts

Attending to the thoughts of others consumes much of our time. We carry out the projects others have conceived; read the books others have written; take our places in systems designed by others; defer to the needs of our children, parents, or spouses; and silence our opinions to keep peace with our neighbors.

At times, we may be the only ones to pay attention to our thoughts, indeed to even consider that we may have thoughts. We alone can give our thoughts air, bring them out into the light, examine them, and give them room to grow.

We start by giving our thoughts respect. What we think does matter. Our thoughts are not less important than those of the person signing our paychecks or performing our annual medical physical. They don't deserve less care

107

than those of a senator drafting a piece of legislation or of a professor writing a textbook. If it were possible to look eye to eye and talk straight with your thoughts, there should be no doubt you would tell your thoughts, as you would a well-loved child, "You matter to me." As children who know that they are welcomed and loved visit freely, so thoughts become more tangible, evident, and frequent when their arrival and presence is anticipated, appreciated, and nurtured.

She grabbed up the pen and felt the mercy of her thoughts coming quickly, zooming through her head out the pen onto the paper . . . She wrote a lot about what she felt, relishing the joy of her fingers gliding across the page, the sheer relief of communication. After a while she sat back and began to really think hard. Then she wrote again . . .[9]

Louise Fitzhugh, *Harriet the Spy*

Giving written form to thoughts is a concrete way of paying attention to them. It is also a way to untangle and expand them. Sometimes anchoring and examining thoughts through writing is the only way we can discover what we really do think and feel about a subject.

A common temptation when trying to figure out "What do I think?" about an issue is to ask another person, "What do you think?" Or to find a book and learn what that author thinks. It's easy to stop stoking the engine of our own thought and instead hitch a ride on someone else's. Someone who seems to have a faster, shinier, more direct train. But we need to sweat and strain to stoke our own engines. To stay with the question, "What do I think?"

and ask, "What do *you* think?" only when we are ready to make a comparison.

"Might isn't Right, is it, Merlyn?"

"Aha!" replied the magician, beaming. "Aha! You are a cunning lad, Arthur, but you won't catch your old tutor like that. You are trying to put me in a passion by making me do the thinking. But I am not to be caught. I am too old a fox for that. You will have to think the rest yourself. Is might right—and if not, why not, give reasons and draw a plan. Besides, what are you going to do about it?"[10]

T. H. White, *The Once and Future King*

Your mind is filled with thoughts. Pay attention to them. Examine them. Some of your thoughts may be less substantial than you would like or than you had believed. Knowing this allows you to bolster them with additional reflection or study. On the other hand, many of your thoughts are likely to be so amazing and beautiful that to go for one minute without paying attention to them would be an irretrievable loss to you and those your life impacts.

9

TRUTH

A Sometimes Skeptic: Part 1

Sometimes, to be a thinker is to be a skeptic. That is, from time to time, to look at what you hold to be true or not true and ask yourself questions about the validity of your verdicts. I'm not suggesting becoming a chronic skeptic who never holds a conviction about anything; I'm suggesting *not* becoming the sort of person who holds a conviction about a great many things but without question or scrutiny.

To revisit the questions—What do I hold as true? What do I hold as untrue?—is like a periodic medical checkup you have not because you assume that your present good health is a farce, but because you want to be prudent. You want assurance that everything is fine; you want to catch anything that is wrong before it gets too far wrong. You don't want to someday hear the words, "If only we had caught this sooner . . . " in regard to your health, any more than you want to admit someday, "How could I have missed that?" in regard to the things you hold as either true or untrue.

Somewhere in you there was something that loved truth, and if ever you studied anything you'd better study that now. For perhaps you won't get another chance.[1]

Charles Williams, *The Place of the Lion*

As human beings, we are fallible. We can make mistakes, drift off course. We can gradually confuse subjective opinion with objective truth. We can too easily and too permanently dismiss something very real as impossible to believe. A wrong mental conclusion or an adopted life principle not founded on truth has huge unseen dangerous consequences: It poisons present observations, interpretations, behaviors, actions, beliefs about others and ourselves, and future expectations.

Yet as human beings, we also are blessed with an immense capacity for insight into truth. Created in God's image with strong minds and intended for relationship with him, we are designed to be receptacles of discovered and revealed truth. As we mature, gather knowledge, and grow in relationship with God, we become increasingly suited for expanded visions of truth, like a graduate student who with added maturity revisits things learned years ago, with eyes now opened to a far greater depth of understanding.

They were all fitting into place, the jig-saw pieces . . . It seemed incredible to me now that I had never understood . . .

111

I had built up false pictures in my mind and sat before them.
I had never had the courage to demand the truth.[2]

Daphne du Maurier, *Rebecca*

A Sometimes Skeptic: Part 2

The goal in being a sometimes skeptic is to grow further in understanding truth. These three questions may help guide you in being a sometimes skeptic:

Question 1: What is the effect of my personal preferences and experiences on my perception of truth?

Is it true? Is it a certainty? Is it real? These are the questions to be asked about matters of belief. *Not,* Do I like this? Does this make me feel good about myself? Will this make my life more comfortable? Will this be useful to me?

Such questions are not without purpose, but they do not help us know truth. After truth is affirmed, then one can honestly ask questions such as, Do I like this? or Does it make me feel good? The answer may be yes or no, but the object of truth remains true nonetheless. Flannery O'Connor wrote, "The truth does not change according to our ability to stomach it emotionally."[3]

Was it wisdom? Was it knowledge? Was it, once more, the deceptiveness of beauty, so that all one's perceptions, half-way to truth, were tangled in a golden mesh?[4]

Virginia Woolf, *To the Lighthouse*

Question 2: On what basis am I calling something true or untrue?

What do we erroneously accept as true? Singular first-hand experience extrapolated to everyone and everything? Our own unchecked interpretations of events and facts? Information from a bad source?

Truth must be referenced to fact, grounded in something. The tower of truth will tumble if it is built on a false foundation. The foundational truth must be established and verified before building on it.

A key strategy for examining foundational truth is to seek a primary source, the source of origin, and verify it there. Don't go to a placard, a neighbor, or a paraphrased brochure. In this era of heavily processed information, we tend to get information from secondary rather than primary sources. We read editorials for or against gun control but don't study the Second Amendment. We discuss the future of the electoral college after listening to shoppers interviewed for the evening news instead of studying the Constitution. We read political writings on abortion rather than studying embryology. We learn about Jesus Christ from books written about him instead of reading his own words in the Gospels.

"What proof," said Ransom (who indeed did feel frightened), "what proof have you that you are being guided or supported by anything except your own individual mind and other people's books?"[5]

C. S. Lewis, *Perelandra*

Question 3: Is this truth in its purest form?

About the commands of God that Moses gave his people, he warned, "Do not add to what I command you and do not subtract from it . . . "[6] Pure truth—without impurities—was insisted upon.

Think of truth as distilled water. Distilled water has been evaporated away from all the impurities and is simply pure water. Distilled truth means the truth itself has been separated from all impurities. Only and exactly truth remains.

The Challenge

Scientists design and conduct experiments. When an experiment is finished, scientists look at the results, form conclusions, and then usually try to publish their findings. Once the findings are made public, other scientists can try the same experiment and see if they get the same result. They also study and analyze what the first scientists did and look for any problems or errors that would invalidate their findings.

It should be no surprise then that scientists are very sure to critique their own work before letting the rest of the scientific community do it for them. They perform checks and double checks, as well as statistical and logistical analyses to make sure their findings will stand up to scrutiny. It is a known fact that certain problems can't be avoided in experiments, so these problems are carefully described in a scientific paper as "limitations" so that a reader of the paper knows that such limitations may add a cautionary note to the conclusions of the paper.

"But how shall we prove anything?"

"We never shall. We can never expect to prove anything upon such a point. It is a difference of opinion which does not admit of proof. We each begin, probably, with a little bias towards our own sex; and upon that bias build every circumstance in favour of it which has occurred within our own circle."[7]

Jane Austen, *Persuasion*

What if we regarded the conclusions we make in life as the stuff of a scientific paper, not with an eye toward statistics and rigid analyses, but with an eye toward an internal check on our own thinking, on our own methods of discovery and subsequent conclusions? Like a scientist, in the quiet of one's own mind, testing a conclusion before stating it, looking for potential challenges. After all, why wait for public questions before asking private questions? Why wait for someone to point out an error before discovering it on our own, or before learning to defend what—in error—is called an error?

Those of us who aren't scientists don't have to expose our theories to worldwide review. But there may be some advantages to this critique-yourself-before-others-do type of review that we can borrow from science.

Instead of being afraid of challenges or unanswered questions, you can diffuse the fear by being the first to pose them to yourself. When you face the questions, challenges, or contrary observations, they become a legitimate object of thought rather than attack. You then can go about the business of finding answers and solutions, knowing that you are involved in an honest struggle to find truth.

You may find too many contradictions, too many questions without answers. You may choose to drop an idea, change an opinion, reexamine an aspect of your faith. You may find you don't know where to look for the answers and may have to ask for help. Or you may find yourself strengthened by the reassuring answers you do discover. Regardless, the process will have shown you how to examine your ideas from many perspectives and how to communicate those ideas to others who may have the same questions.

Facts Transformed

The facts of nighttime dreams are random, without context, unlinked to reality, meaningless. This happens and then that happens without apparent connection. In the morning we wake up, remember our dreams, and wonder, *Where did that come from?*

In contrast, the facts of waking reality are neither isolated nor random. They exist within a real-life context. Examined within that context, an apparent fact is transformed into another and takes on meaning.

For example, consider the fact that a stick of butter (1/4 lb.) contains eight hundred calories of pure fat. A stick of butter and the calories it contains are detrimental to a dieter but life-giving to an arctic trekker. Likewise, to a preliterate child, words on pages are meaningless marks; to the interested reader, a source of delight.

Thinking requires the gathering and use of facts. But thinking isn't complete if the facts that we gather and use are not considered within the context of reality. Moreover, our thinking is unfinished until we consider facts within the context of the reality of God's created order. Considered within this context, facts are viewed through and transformed by God's lens.

*If it had ever occurred to her to question whether all these
things might be the reality behind what she had been taught
at school as "religion," she had put the thought aside.*[8]

C. S. Lewis, *That Hideous Strength*

Thomas Kelly writes in *Testament of Devotion,*

Facts remain facts, when brought into the Presence in
the deeper level, but their value, their significance, is
wholly realigned. Much apparent wheat becomes utter
chaff, and some chaff becomes wheat. Imposing powers?
They are out of the Life, and must crumble. Lost causes?
If God be for them, who can be against them? Rationally
plausible futures? They are weakened or certified in the
dynamic Life and Light. Tragic suffering? Already He is
there, and we actively move, in His tenderness, toward
the sufferers. Hopeless debauchees? These are children
of God, His concern and ours. Inexorable laws of nature? The dependable framework for divine reconstruc-
tion. The fall of a sparrow? The Father's love. For faith
and hope and love for all things are engendered in the
soul . . . as we humbly see all things, even darkly and as
through a glass, yet through the eye of God.[9]

Transforming facts in such a manner is not about being
blind or naive, as if the goal is a "live happily ever after"
facade in the midst of difficulty or suffering. It is not about
putting an artificial positive spin on a situation. The words
"Everything will turn out fine" may stick in the throat
while sitting in an emergency room awaiting news on a
son who may not recover, because in fact, everything may
turn out very badly. But instead of these hollow words,
God's higher truth allows the startling revelation to enter
the mind that the divine hands that hold the son on earth
can just as sturdily hold the son in heaven. The venue of

the son forever changed, the care of the son constant. A fact transformed.

"It means," said Aslan, ". . . there is a magic deeper still . . ."[10]
C. S. Lewis, *The Lion, the Witch, and the Wardrobe*

Consider how the facts of our sleepy dreamy lives are transformed in the context of a world created by a God who says about those he has created, "I have loved you with an everlasting love,"[11] and who says about himself, "Who is my equal?"[12]

10

QUESTIONS AND ANSWERS

Prelude to Answers

In college, a certain chemistry topic left me so confused that I knew it was beyond the limit of my unaided comprehension. I had to talk with my professor. But how could he explain it to me if I didn't understand it well enough even to tell him what I didn't understand?

I needed to be able to "name" what I didn't understand before going to him. I could hope to do this only by trying to isolate my confusion by writing and rewriting questions, trying to get them more and more specific. As I did, an amazing thing happened: I began to understand. When I finally brought my page of questions to my professor, I understood. He needed only to confirm that I did.

The lesson from chemistry class? Questions are the prelude to answers. As such, they require careful cultivation and attention. Working to ask questions from a basis of insight, rather than confusion, prepares your mind for the answers.

In keeping with the spirit of a liberal arts education, that lesson in crafting questions has stayed with me considerably longer than my understanding of the chemistry topic in question. Although the lesson is remembered, the challenge remains to apply it.

Our lives are full of questions, many of which are as confusing as anything from chemistry class. With stakes higher than a grade, the incentive to ask questions, good questions that set our minds in motion and move us toward answers, is high.

> *"The rains are best for you?" She asked: she had a keen desire to learn. The Reform Bill and Senlac and a little French lay like treasure trove in her brain. She expected answers to every question, and she absorbed them hungrily.*[1]
>
> Graham Greene, *The Power and the Glory*

Good questions take time to form, time to find the words that will bring the vague inner sense of wonder or discomfort from the abstract to the concrete. Good questions require soul searching: Am I asking because I really want to know, regardless of what I find?

The questions we ask have everything to do with the way we think things are. Just as a hypothesis in an experiment may be based on a hunch that proves invalid after laborious study, a question also may be based on an invalid assumption. In that case, time spent searching for an answer might have been better spent getting the question right.

A wrong question also may arise from ignorance where there should be knowledge. Jesus rejected the premise of his questioners—"You are in error"[2]—on the basis that they did not know the Scriptures. They were asking the wrong question because they didn't know what they should have known.

Not all questions can be answered in this lifetime. And some questions are themselves the result of prolonged pondering and in their unanswered state are almost a form of conclusion. Nevertheless, thoughtfully forming and asking questions actively invests you in the process of discovery.

The Blue-Book Exam

If Jesus were the professor of a class in which we were students, and if he were to pass out an exam, my bet is that it would be a blue-book exam.

The blue-book exam gained its name from the characteristic blue paper cover stapled around a stack of blank lined paper. The booklet merely gives shape and form to the essay test. In this booklet, the student writes his or her answer to one or more questions posed by the professor. Sometimes the answer to a single question fills an entire blue book.

The blue-book exam leaves one's mind naked before the professor. There is no hope of getting a multiple-choice question correct just by guessing. No chance of deducing the correct fill-in-the-blank word based on the context of the other words. If one had the mind to cheat, a quick look at a neighbor's blue book would reveal only line after line of handwriting, not a concrete answer one could snatch and record as one's own.

121

A student simply has no choice but to start thinking and writing. One has to find within oneself something with which to fill the pages. Based on this knowledge and those memorized facts, using that reasoning skill, one must synthesize an answer: "This is what I think."

How does a blue-book exam relate to Jesus? In the Gospels of Matthew, Mark, Luke, and John, Jesus asked many provocative questions. Important questions that, if taken seriously, forced those who were questioned to think hard. Like any teacher, he based his questions on material his students should have studied, lectures to which they had listened, demonstrations they had observed, and stories they had discussed.

Imagine we are the students in the class taught by Jesus. The pages of the blue books before us are open and empty. Our pencils are sharpened. Here are the professor's questions as he asked them nearly two millennia ago:

- "Who do you say I am?"[3]
- "What good will it be for a man if he gains the whole world, yet forfeits his soul? Or what can a man give in exchange for his soul?"[4]
- "What do you want me to do for you?"[5]
- "What do you think about the Christ? Whose son is he?"[6]
- "Which is greater: the gift, or the altar that makes the gift sacred?"[7]

Getting to the Answer

The most important thing to do with a good question is obvious: Try to answer it. For the easy-answer question, this is not a problem. But the tough questions leave us in a quandary. These questions can't be answered by looking up facts. They require flashes of insight, uncovered connections between facts, the work of reason in cooperation with faith.

Let me suggest three guiding principles for starting on the tough questions. First, start somewhere. Second, build on what you know. Third, aim to make at least an informed guess, eventually.

The suggestion "Start somewhere" is hardly profound, but the effects of starting can be profound—like placing a vase of fresh flowers on a table in a messy house can be the first, but defining, act in a long process of putting things right. By taking the first step to answer a tough question, one's energy is directed toward a single point instead of dissipated throughout the large vastness of all that is unknown.

> *People often ask themselves the right questions. Where they fail is in answering the questions they ask themselves, and even there they do not fail by much. A single avenue of reasoning followed to its logical conclusions would bring them straight home to the truth. But they stop just short of it, over and over again. When they have only to reach out and grasp the idea that would explain everything, they decide that the search is hopeless.*[8]
>
> William Maxwell, *Time Will Darken It*

A story in the Gospel of Matthew tells of religious leaders who question Jesus about his miracles: "By what authority are you doing these things?"[9]

Jesus answers by directing a question back to them: "John's baptism—where did it come from? Was it from heaven, or from men?" You answer my question, he tells them, then I'll answer yours.

The religious leaders form a huddle and debate. Their response: "We don't know."

Ignorance was their strategy; they admitted nothing on which to base an answer. Consequently, Jesus ignored their question.

One of the many things that can be learned from this story is that if we want answers, we have to be willing to start somewhere. Maybe if the religious leaders had answered with anything truthful and honest, either they would have been given, or they would have themselves realized, the answer to their original question.

No doubt, the religious leaders did know something about Jesus' question with which they could have begun to formulate an answer. Each of us already knows a vast amount about whatever issues our questions relate to. If we listed all that we already knew, we would probably be overcome by our personal genius. This abundance of banked knowledge can be put to good use.

Go back in your mind and rediscover a trick learned in high school geometry when you set out to prove such mathematical truths as the hypotenuse of a triangle is less than the sum of its two opposite sides. In setting up a geometric proof, you started with what you knew and worked toward what you did not. Step-by-step, you combined what you knew with an established principle to allow you to take your knowledge to the next step. If this, then that; then if that, then this. And so on and so on.

Applying this to real life, go as far down through the unknown as needed to find a truth. Or pick one of many truths you already know. Even if it is a most basic truth: "I am a human being," or "In the beginning, God created the heavens and the earth." C. S. Lewis began his search for ultimate meaning in life with the simple fact that he had joy.[10]

A tough question can lead you into rich enough thought territory to keep you thinking and wondering for a long time. As fruitful as this ongoing process can be, however, don't lose sight of the fact that ultimately you do want an answer to your question. At least a partial answer, if a full one seems impossible. So make it your goal to eventually make an informed guess as to what the answer might be.

Such an informed guess is called a hypothesis. A hypothesis is not a conclusion; it is not the answer. It is simply a good guess, which remains to be either proven or disproven. This is the basis of all scientific experiments. As an experiment unfolds to show certain aspects of a hypothesis false, but other aspects of a hypothesis intact, the scientist adapts the hypothesis and continues with experiments to further refine the hypothesis. These refinements move toward an ultimate answer or discovery, a process that can't occur without an initial informed guess.

"Look here," said the great man, good-humouredly, "you've no business to be asking how I guessed right. You ought to be guessing at the guesses yourselves. Think it out." [11]

G. K. Chesterton, "The White Pillars Murder"

Primed with Knowledge

Look up into a clear night sky. Let your eyes scan the blanket of stars. If you are in the Northern Hemisphere, can you find the constellation Cassiopeia? If you are in the Southern Hemisphere, the Southern Cross? If you have never before seen your hemisphere's respective constellation or if you don't know the pattern of its stars, you likely will not find it. If, however, you have seen it before or know the pattern of its stars, your eyes know what to look for. In fact, once you have seen one constellation, you can more easily find another, even one you've never seen before, because your eyes can more easily recognize any pattern of stars after they have seen one.

> *He gazed about him, and the very intensity of his desire to take in the new world at a glance defeated itself. He saw nothing but colours—colours that refused to form themselves into things. Moreover, he knew nothing yet well enough to see it; you cannot see things till you know roughly what they are.*[12]
>
> C. S. Lewis, *Out of the Silent Planet*

A base of knowledge, even beginning knowledge, helps us make ongoing discoveries. A cook with some experience can recognize a good recipe even before preparing it. A newly married man can recognize his wife's blood relatives at an extended-family reunion by their common facial features. A trained hematologist can detect evidence of disease in a cell under her microscope's lens, when such a cell would seem only a blob to an untrained eye.

Whatever present knowledge or understanding you have is like a magnet for more. It is like toothpicks holding your eyes open to see more, or a treasure map leading you to discover more.

Antiquarian book dealers Leona Rostenberg and Madeleine Stern have acquired a great deal of knowledge about rare and valuable books in their experience of over half a century. In fact, their knowledge is so deeply ingrained that their ability to recognize rarity and value in a book has become almost instinctual. In their book *Old Books, Rare Friends,* Rostenberg and Stern call this sixth sense afforded by knowledge "Finger-Spitzengefühl."[13] As this term apparently implies, they sometimes experience this recognition of rarity and value as an actual tingling in the fingertips. Their investment in knowledge has earned them this unique internal recognition and messaging system. They know better than to let such messages go unheeded.

By wisdom a house is built,

and through understanding it is established;

through knowledge its rooms are filled

with rare and beautiful treasures.[14]

From the Book of Proverbs

The person infused with knowledge recognizes the valuable, the rare, and the beautiful. The treasures of life motion from the shelf when eyes of knowledge pass, whispering, "This is what you must discover. This is what you must find."

Unexpected Discovery

The discovery of penicillin by Sir Alexander Fleming is a classic tale of serendipity.[15] *Serendipity* is a word for the phenomenon of finding something unsought while looking for something else.

In 1928, Fleming inoculated culture plates with staphylococci bacteria before leaving for vacation. Upon return to his London laboratory, he saw that mold had contaminated the plates and so he placed the contaminated plates in a discard pile. An astute assistant, however, looked at the plates before tossing them. Noticing that the staphylococci bacteria were not growing around the mold, he alerted Fleming. Fleming tested the mold growth and found that the mold produced a chemical that killed the bacteria. That chemical is now known as penicillin.

Fleming claimed, "Penicillin happened . . . It came out of the blue." But what had Fleming done to prepare the way for the discovery? He was actively working, researching, experimenting, thinking. When his observant assistant showed him the killed staphylococci, Fleming knew how to proceed. He identified the mold, engaged other researchers to study it, and analyzed the antibacterial effect of the bright yellow chemical released by the mold into the culture plates. A series of chance events greeted Fleming, but he knew what to do and did it.

He stared into the sink. "An infantile dream. Of course I know that. Fleming discovered penicillin by an inspired accident. But an accident has to be inspired. An old second-rate doctor would never have an accident like that, but it was no business of theirs—was it?—if I wanted to dream."[16]

Graham Greene, *Our Man in Havana*

Unexpected discoveries can occur for any of us. They are like the visit of a miracle on a busy, alert mind. How can you welcome such a visit? Be expectant. Be active: doing, seeking, praying, thinking. Be alert to the unforeseen. Pay attention to anything that "jumps out at you": a newspaper article, a story or ad on TV, a comment from a friend or stranger, a phrase in a book, a book on a shelf, a jarring circumstance, a coincidence. Ask questions: Does this fit with anything I'm working on or thinking about? Does this fit with anything else unexpected I've encountered? What might be the significance?

Recognize a discovery, new direction, or opportunity, and be ready to take it further.

Brooding

On the way, Nancy did not talk much. She was mulling over the various angles to the mystery.[7]

Carolyn Keene, *The Mystery of the 99 Steps*

Brooding is intense thought dedicated to a specific object of thought—such as a question or problem—over a prolonged period of time. Brooding implies a high level of intimacy between the thought and the object, such that for a time there seems an inseparable quality between the two. One's mind stays with the object. Whether at a desk or at the hairdresser, whether researching at the library or lying on a beach chair at the shore, one's mind holds the object.

Brooding can be directed toward the question or problem to be answered or solved as a whole. Or it can take the form of a more focused meditation on a word or words that make up the question or problem, or on the ideas that wrap themselves around the question or problem,

129

or on the positive result that is anticipated (that is, the problem solved, the question answered). Brooding can link the question or problem with prayer or relevant passages of Scripture. Pondering such a linked pair invites divine informing to the process.

The unfolding of your words gives light.[18]

From the Book of Psalms

The link between blanketing something with attention and achieving creative results is literally as old as time. In the same breath as "In the beginning . . . ," the writer of Genesis reports that "the Spirit of God was hovering over the waters."[19] These words conjure up images of dwelling and lingering over the primordial waters. Transfer this image to an object of chaos or confusion set before you that you are trying to resolve or bring to order. Brood—hover, linger, dwell—over that object with your mind's presence. Examine it at length with your mind's eye.

A moment comes when the undifferentiated mass over which you are brooding appears to stabilize to the point at which it is no longer sloshing and uncontained but rather a mass of substance allowing handling—like a pancake whose batter is now baked sufficiently to be flipped. This moment of mental congealing is a good sign that your brooding may soon be rewarded with insight or discovery.

Thought—to call it by a prouder name than it deserved— had let its line down into the stream. It swayed, minute after minute, hither and thither among the reflections and the weeds, letting the water lift it and sink it, until—you know the little tug—the sudden conglomeration of an idea at the end of one's line: and then the cautious hauling of it in, and the careful laying of it out?[20]

Virginia Woolf, *A Room of One's Own*

Finding

Once begun and attended to, the process of asking a question and seeking an answer will eventually have results. The result we set out wanting most—an answer to the question—may not be the result most forthcoming, however. Along the way from question to answer, more questions, as well as answers begging their own questions, will emerge. New insights into one's personal ways of thinking and new skills in asking and seeking will also emerge. All these are the firstfruits of the asking-seeking cycle.

The answer that was the focus of the initial question may be quick or slow in appearing. What we need is not to keep an eye on the clock, but to have a determination to continue to do the things that better our chances of intercepting the answer: ponder, brood, study, pray, pay attention.

And then it happened—the thing he had been half-unconsciously expecting . . . He remembered—not one thing, nor another thing, nor a logical succession of things, but everything—the whole thing, perfect, complete, in all its dimensions as it were and instantaneously; as if he stood outside the world and saw it suspended in infinitely

131

dimensional space. He no longer needed to reason about it, or even to think about it. He knew it.[21]

Dorothy L. Sayers, *Whose Body?*

Some answers come as an "aha"-type insight. For example, one awakens in the morning knowing the answer to a question struggled with the night before. Or a new and clear insight about a mess of a problem shines clear while one washes the car. Although "aha" answers may come at different times and in different ways, what they have in common is that they typically follow a period of concentrated thought, often significant amounts of concentrated thought.

In contrast to the "aha" solution, the answer may, over a period of time, be untangled from within a web of accumulated facts and ideas. The detangler may be a sequence of logical thought followed from beginning to end, a gradual ruling out of all but what stands as true, a divine sense of discernment between more than one reasonable answer, or a meticulous study of all the facts and ideas leading to a solution that stands up to reasonable scrutiny.

It took me fifteen minutes to jot down the facts as I remembered them, one piece of information per card until I'd exhausted my store. I laid them out on my desk, rearranging the order, shuffling them into columns, looking for connections I hadn't seen before.[22]

Sue Grafton, *"M" Is for Malice*

The answer may continue to elude you. You may find that your initial question needs to be revised. You may find an answer to a question you didn't ask but which makes your initial question irrelevant. You may be tempted to close out the question with a less-than-satisfactory answer or to just give it up. You may also discover that unanswered questions can add richness to life when they prompt an ongoing attitude of seeking and anticipation.

11

STRETCH AND STRAIN

A Willingness to Be Perplexed

Why must holy places be dark places?[1]

C. S. Lewis, *Till We Have Faces*

God apparently is willing to allow mystery, to leave us confused, to let some questions go unanswered. Why else would the nature of the Trinity be so elusive, the details of creation so sketchy, the exchange of Christ's blood for our free and eternal lives so anti–common sense?

There appears to be some cap to the accessible revelation of the knowledge of the universe—that is, this and no more can be fully understood by humankind. Whether this cap is universal for everyone or permanent for all of time, who can know? On a more micro level, there is also a cap to each of our individual capacities for understanding. Whether due to will, genetics, environment, or some mystery factor, each of us can figure out or understand only so much. Should it then be any surprise that all of us live with unanswered questions?

> *There are years that ask questions and years that answer.*[2]
> Zora Neale Hurston, *Their Eyes Were Watching God*

Most of us don't like unanswered questions. Like cold water to a burn, so an answer is to a question. It quenches, relieves, stops the discomfort.

Yet it is a fact that many of our most pressing questions may have no answer quickly forthcoming, or even in the foreseeable future. And it can be a mistake to rush to patch a difficult question with a false answer, however soothing that answer may at first be.

> *"And were the opportunity to come to you," I said, "what would you say . . . Why does God allow humans to suffer?" . . .*
>
> *I believe that had she answered in any other way—had she attempted, for example, to foist upon me some pat piety, some fraudulent platitude, had she recited a list of reasons for suffering . . . had she tried, in Milton's words, "to justify the*

135

ways of God to man,"—I would have rejected her soundly, once and for all.

She grimaced, however, and shook her head sadly. "Oh Margaret, honey, I don't know exactly how to answer that," she said. "I don't know why . . ."[3]

Jamie Langston Turner, *Some Wildflower in My Heart*

The alternative to rushing to judgment is patience, a commitment to thinking and prayer, and perhaps most difficult, a willingness to be uncomfortable. Philosopher and educator John Dewey wrote, "Reflective thinking is always more or less troublesome because it involves . . . willingness to endure a condition of mental unrest and disturbance. Reflective thinking, in short, means judgment suspended during further inquiry; and suspense is likely to be somewhat painful."[4]

We can be so averse to discomfort, so taken with trying to find the arc that will take us from where we are (i.e., the question) to the end point (i.e., the answer), that we don't see, explore, or discover all that may lie along or under that arc. By transferring our focus to discovering what we can, to thinking thoroughly about possible answers, to being content with what remains mysterious, we commit ourselves to truth rather than answers.

A willingness to be perplexed is a claim on a future answer that is more than a slice of the "maybe" truth. It is a claim on an answer that your mind has wrestled with, wrapped itself around, and owned in understanding.

Practice saying, "I don't know." Resolve to relax the tightness that arises in your throat or gut when asked a question for which your quick answer has an apparently obvious loophole. Exchange the tightness with an openness to the ongoing search for all that is true.

The Simple, the Complex

In an article entitled *The Good Doctor*, Pulitzer Prize-winning author Tracy Kidder tells the story of Dr. Paul Farmer, a Harvard-educated medical doctor who lives among the poor in Haiti, serving them with his gift of healing.[5] The scenario is simple. On the one hand, the poor in Haiti are sick. They are dying, particularly of AIDS and tuberculosis. On the other hand, Farmer knows how to heal the sick and care for the dying. He knows how to treat AIDS and tuberculosis. Although it appears to be a simple match of need and provision, it is not.

In order for Farmer's provision to meet the needs of the sick Haitian poor, he has to navigate layer upon layer of economic, political, sociologic, religious, medical, and civic barriers as he manages the synergistic issues of poverty, hunger, suffering, belief in sorcery, problems of land use, poor sanitation, inadequate housing, and more. All these issues have a direct effect on the spread of disease, the availability of drugs, the willingness and ability of the people to submit and adhere to treatment, and the ultimate efficacy of treatment.

His brain adjusted itself achingly from the phrase "so happy" to the phrase "do not trust." He said, "What are you talking about, Yusef?" He could feel the mechanism of his brain creaking, grinding, scraping, cogs failing to connect, all with pain.[6]

Graham Greene, *The Heart of the Matter*

Many things in life appear clear and simple but aren't. Layers of complexity are common. For example, consider issues that are presented as black and white: This person is right and that person is wrong; to be at work is better than to be at home, or vice versa; option A is cheaper than option B; this church or that school is the place to be. Yet it is likely that not one of those issues is as simple as the statement implies. Another example: The way to resolve a dispute seems clear—just work it out. But those words and that goal often float on the surface of deep and turbulent waters.

The questions we have, as well as the tasks set before us, often can't be resolved until we have gone deep below the surface and thought hard, sometimes harder than we care to or believe possible. A subject may be so difficult or complex that just as one begins to approach some level of understanding, a mental circuit trips and one's thought is thrown a distance. Resting on comfortable assumptions or generic conclusions is understandably a tempting substitute for pushing oneself to go deeper, just as falling back on singing the melody is tempting after straining to pick up a harmony line.

It's a fascinating case. Every piece of evidence can point either way, depending on how you choose to look at it. I can lie awake at night thinking about it. It ought to be compulsory study for every detective constable, a warning of how a case can go wrong if the police get it fixed in their minds that it has to be the husband.[7]

P. D. James, *The Skull Beneath the Skin*

The goal is not to make everything difficult and daunting, to perceive so much of the complexity at the beginning as to be discouraged from going further. Although we don't want to be shallow, trite, or simplistic, we also don't want

138

to be overwhelmed, pessimistic, or defeated. The goal is to cultivate an appreciation of the complexity represented by any single seemingly simple conclusion, question, decision, belief, or goal. And then to go beyond this appreciation and be willing to struggle through that complexity, as needed, so as to arrive at the end point—whether an end point of thought or action—with integrity.

To See the Whole

An unknown number of years before Christ was born, God prepared the Garden of Eden for his premier man and woman . . . Two thousand years after God transcribed his laws to Moses, his grace reached a pinnacle with the sacrifice of his Son . . . At the time of the early church, the Spirit of God led the apostle Paul to write with steady clarity the expectations of Christian conduct . . . Centuries earlier, the same Spirit had led a king ("a man after [God's] own heart"[8]), whose behavior was often not a model of godly conduct, to write with passion of the extreme peaks and valleys of human experience . . . Pages and pages of the Old Testament record an angry God speaking of vengeance toward and judgment of his wayward people . . . Pages and pages of the New Testament record a loving Christ dining with sinners, healing bleeding and blindness, cradling children, washing feet, and then finally dying on behalf of all the wayward people.

All this and more is God. The nature of his creation, the apparent paradoxes, the range of actions and expectations, the tension between mercy and justice, love and holiness. We can barely begin to comprehend it all as one picture. The picture of God is larger than any Bible story we remember as a child or any verse we bring to mind when trouble

139

comes. The whole picture of God is outside the ownership of any one Christian tradition or political party, is beyond the eloquent narrative of any single popular author, and can't be contained within one descriptive attribute.

> *"Remember, young man, unceasingly," Father Païssy began, without preface, "after . . . cruel analysis the learned of this world have nothing left of all that was sacred of old. But they have only analyzed the parts and overlooked the whole, and indeed their blindness is marvellous. Yet the whole still stands steadfast before their eyes, and the gates of hell shall not prevail against it."[9]*
>
> Fyodor Dostoevsky, *Brothers Karamazov*

The relevance of the whole picture of God is not limited to within the walls of the church or the halls in which theology is studied or the bedroom in which his follower prays. The relevance of the whole picture of God sinks down deep into his created order. Into science and business and veterinary medicine and theater arts and plumbing. Into the green of the cedars and the red plumage of the cardinal and the turquoise waters of the Florida Keys. Into the people he created, whose lives are complex, for whom sorrow is deep yet joy soars. Into every place and every thing.

The whole picture is more than what we can see or know or understand: Mystery exists. Miracles happen. Death haunts us, but has somehow been defeated. Life is eternal. Dependence on God is universal; God is all powerful; God needs us and loves us. There are so many strokes to the picture of God, to the picture of what and whom he has created.

12

LIFELONG LEARNING

A Right to Learn

Listening to two professional educators casually discuss learning temporarily froze me. How could I write or comment with integrity on thought and learning when I had never even heard of the expert one of them had just quoted or didn't know the premise of modern education on which they were nodding their heads in agreement? After all, what are my credentials? Only a bachelor's degree in biology. What right did I have to venture into their field?

Similarly, what of a woman with an associate in arts degree who wishes to understand physics? Or a man with a high school diploma who wants to explore political science? Or a music professor who is intrigued by medicine?

How can any one of us who is not an expert in a field of interest pursue that interest without trespassing on property purchased by others?

What knowledge do we have the right to explore?

And the more pictures Novalee took and the more she developed, the more she wanted to learn about what she was doing. She studied photography magazines—Camera & Darkroom and the Photo Review. She made calls to photo labs in Sacramento, California, and wrote letters to Kodak in Rochester, New York.[1]

Billie Letts, *Where the Heart Is*

After unfreezing myself from the paralysis of educational inferiority, I reassured myself that anyone can pursue anything. Not just anyone can be an expert, of course, but anyone can be an interested, informed participant in any field.

As I warmed further to my educational acceptability, I reasoned that although the role of an interested, informed participant is obviously quite different from that of an expert, it may be just as significant. After all, although I'm not an expert on learning or thinking, I am a learner and a thinker. I can report on what I observe and read and learn and discover in my life, as surely as the expert can report on what she observes in the classroom, learns from study, or reads in academic journals. My recorded interest doesn't change the material taught or learned in academic settings as an expert's would, but it does document the practical struggle for solid thought and learning of the nonacademic, nonexpert mind. In other words, the struggle of an everyday woman living everyday life.

And what of the woman interested in physics who never took a class in quantum theory? To think and possibly write about how she sees the world in a new way due to an understanding of physics is exciting and valid. And what of the man interested in political science who never took a course in public policy or attended law school? Politics from the perspective of a voter and a taxpayer is as valid a framework for thought as politics from the viewpoint of the candidate or incumbent.

From what platform can you be an active participant in a field, learning, thinking, or speaking about a topic of your interest but not your training? The answer: from the significant platform of an everyday person . . .

- whose life has been helped and enriched by knowing about the topic
- whose world has been broadened by what you have learned
- who understands how the theories and principles worked out at the laboratory bench or in the class-room are affecting your days and future
- who finds joy in your expanding understanding
- who has insights you want to share

Pursuing Self-Education

Mortimer Adler, philosopher, educator, and editor, wrote, "Nothing but a serious illness relieves any adult of his responsibility to continue learning year after year, every part of every year, until the end of his life."[2]

Mr. Adler and my friend Bob would be in perfect agreement. Bob is in his eighties. I've known Bob since I joined the church to which he belongs about twenty years ago. Every Sunday, as he has for all these years of Sundays, he sits pen in hand, filling the margins of bulletins and the pages of notebooks with what he has just learned, with what he wants to remember for the rest of his life.

Self-education can be as uncomplicated as that—putting yourself on a regular basis in a place where you can learn what you need or want to learn. Alternatively, you could add a specific element or structure to your life, such as a class, mentoring relationship, or designated study plan.

> *The library was a little old shabby place. Francie thought it was beautiful . . . Francie thought that all the books in the world were in that library and she had a plan about reading all the books in the world. She was reading a book a day in alphabetical order and not skipping the dry ones . . . She had been reading a book a day for a long time now and she was still in the B's. Already she had read about bees and buffaloes, Bermuda vacations and Byzantine architecture.*[3]
>
> Betty Smith, *A Tree Grows in Brooklyn*

What shall you learn about? Choose something that sparks your interest or about which you are regrettably ignorant. Choose something that moves you further along a life of wisdom and truth, that brings you joy, that helps you answer the questions of your life, that is fun.

If you are putting yourself in charge of finding material to study, you may find it challenging to think back to the days of gathering references for a term paper. Here is a brief refresher: Choose a book or article about your subject of interest. That book or article will provide terms and names of experts in the field you can use to search for more books or articles using the library catalogs or to do a Web search. If there is ongoing research about your topic, you likely will come across the name of leading research institutions, which could provide more information. Also look up the subject in the *Gale Directory of Publications and Broadcast Media* (available at most libraries) for names of specific periodicals dedicated to that subject. Like links in a chain, this term connects you with that name, connects you with this institution, connects you with that discovery, connects you with this book, and so on, and so on.

Soon scaffold points—themes and basic principles—of the subject will become evident. You will begin to see a historical perspective and discover the questions that fuel ongoing thought, discussion, or research within the field. You will also develop questions of your own that will fuel your personal ongoing study. Maybe you will want to seek out other individuals with a similar interest with whom you can meet for discussion.

Keep reading, studying, digesting. Squish it in, level it off, pack it down, add more. Repeat until rich and dense.

Our Absent Teachers

Again quoting from Mortimer Adler: "For those of us who are no longer in school . . . it is necessary, if we want to go on learning and discovering, to know how to make books teach us well."[4] In his classic, *How to Read a Book*, Adler shows his readers how to do exactly what the title of the book indicates. One of the first hurdles he surmounts is helping his readers answer the question, Which books should we choose to be our "absent teachers"?

This is an important question. After all, how do we look beyond the prescribed monthly book club selection arriving in the mail; discern the books of value from among those lining the shelves at the library; or glean the pearls from the multitude of titles at the local bookstore, many of which are compelling when taken down, dust-free, from a paneled shelf and thumbed through while seated in an overstuffed chair?

According to Adler, the key to choosing a book from which to learn is prereading, or what he calls "systematic skimming."[5] Read the front and back covers and inside flaps. Look over the preface and introduction. Study the table of contents and the index, if there is one. Watch for key words and topics that are of interest. Look up some passages related to those topics or key words. How does it seem so far?

Read a couple summary statements at the beginning or end of chapters. Read the first few pages and, if it's a nonfiction book, the last few. Spot check the book by reading several paragraphs or pages at random.

Once a book is selected, you must do more than read it if you want it to teach you well. You must be actively engaged with it in what Walt Whitman described as "a gymnast's struggle."[6] Interact with the book. What do you think of the author's conclusion to chapter 1? Do you agree with her main premise in chapter 2? Is the reasoning logical in chapter 8? Is what the author is saying true throughout?

Sent Franklin to Hatchards for copy of War and Peace, *thinking today good time to start long book . . . Silly woman came back with* Anna Karenina, *saying it was the nearest thing she could find. Got as far as first sentence, then stopped to think. "All happy families resemble one another, but each unhappy family is unhappy in its own way." Great author has got that the wrong way round. I think unhappiness is*

*much the same whatever the reasons for it, and happiness is a
quirky odd sort of thing.*[7]
Dorothy L. Sayers and Jill Patton Walsh, *Thrones, Dominations*

Make notes in the margin. Write down your questions
as they arise. Write "Yes!" or "No!" where you agree or disagree with the author. Make note of something else a passage makes you think of or another book in which you've
read something similar. Put brackets around something
you particularly want to remember. Watch for the author
to define her terms. Keep a list of key pages to which you
may want to return.

Use your books as a springboard for personal independent thought, not just as a repository for the thought of
others. Think about the significance of what you've read,
about how it might change you, about how it might change
how you look at the world.

*[Janie] didn't read books so she didn't know that she was the
world and the heavens boiled down to a drop.*[8]
Zora Neale Hurston, *Their Eyes Were Watching God*

Gathered Together

A group of us sat in a circle, taking turns reading aloud
from the book we were studying, *A Serious Call to a Devout
and Holy Life* by William Law. One person held her eyes
shut tight as she listened to the reading; another followed
along down the page, pencil in hand, making notes in the
margins or underlining; another kept flipping through the

Bible to find supporting passages. Several said that it was helpful to read the chapter aloud; another said it was difficult to grasp the meaning while listening. Some seemed unaffected by the writer's words, while others groaned when the message struck deep. How different we all were! Nevertheless, those of us who sat around that circle now share a common knowledge of the message of William Law: that the reason we don't live as we ought to or as we aspire to is that we really don't intend to. Intention makes all the difference. The words *intend* and *intention* became among us shorthand for the challenge represented by that book.

> *They had lived years without me. Now they possessed a language of shared experience in which I was nonexistent. Often they would slip into the shorthand of private signs and notations that form the speech of people who have been together intimately for great lengths of time. There were smiles about the train system from Vienna to Zurich, expressions of wonder at the cleanliness of Switzerland, grimaces over the traffic in Paris.[9]*
>
> Chaim Potok, *My Name Is Asher Lev*

Learning together builds an intimacy among those doing the learning, whether the group is traveling together through Europe, or meeting every Monday night at the community center to discuss foreign travel or quilting, or meeting every Sunday morning during a church education hour. Each person in the group takes on the same new body of knowledge. The knowledge becomes like shared currency, which can then be drawn upon. Individuals can together grapple with questions and share in the search for answers. Each can contribute one's unique knowledge, experience, and insights to the group, further increasing the scope of what each person in the group knows, sees, and understands. A woman who grew up in California can expand the horizon of the woman from Maine, and vice versa. Women and men of different faith backgrounds can show each other how their Christian traditions uniquely shed light on what it means to be a Christian in today's culture. Lessons from the workplace and lessons from the home can be exchanged.

A shared body of knowledge is particularly important to the life of a group whose members have a deep commitment to each other, such as a family, a church congregation, or neighbors. With a shared body of knowledge, the group is made stronger by the uniting force of that knowledge. As one person grows, another person grows, and the group grows, which helps another person grow, and the group grows yet more. As learning together continues, the shared foundation on which the group stands is continually reinforced and the group is strengthened.

"I have not thought very much."

"No. Then let me do some thinking with you."[10]

T. H. White, *The Once and Future King*

The Round Table of Counsel

A central theme in the legend of King Arthur is his Round Table, at which Arthur surrounded himself with the noblest knights in the land. At the table, the knights shared news of their latest adventures and advised the king and one another on matters of mutual kingdom interest.

> *"But, behold now, on this the first day of the Round Table, I lay upon you all the Order of Chivalry. All of you, and those who shall sit afterwards at this Table, are the Knights of Logres, and for the glory of Logres, the Realm of Righteousness, do not ever depart from the high virtues of this realm."*[11]
>
> Roger Lancelyn Green,
> *King Arthur and His Knights of the Round Table*

Despite his power, King Arthur was in the same state as we are: not self-sufficient. We often need to learn from others and be guided by their knowledge, experience, and wisdom. Like Arthur, we would be wise to do some advance planning as to those with whom we will surround ourselves.

In 1945 Lee R. Steiner published *Where Do People Take Their Troubles?* in which she reported the results of an experiment confirming people's propensity to trust bad counsel.[12] In the experiment, the counsel was given by an imposter, yet it was received by seekers, largely without hesitation. Decades later, we may be tempted to believe members of society enlightened, not so desperate for counsel, but the steady stream of letters to newspaper columnists and callers to radio talk shows, as well as the number of faithful readers of horoscopes and dubious self-help books, demonstrates otherwise. At the very least, there is evidence that many of us do not have access to or take advantage of a close company of wise and faithful counsel.

The first and foremost wise and faithful counsel with whom we should align ourselves is God. God's counsel is available to us through Scripture, through the life and continuing presence of Jesus Christ, and through the inner guidance of the Holy Spirit, also known as the "Counselor."

"To God belong wisdom and power;

counsel and understanding are his."[3]

From the Book of Job

But we need wise and faithful people in our lives also. We need friends and family who care about us, want God's highest will for us, and speak words of truth. We also need objective and proven spiritual advisors to counsel and inform us without the tangle of intimate friendship or family bonds. At times we may need to seek out "experts" who can help us by sharing specific knowledge, teaching us a skill, or discerning the nature of and solution to a particular problem. We need to cultivate this virtual round table of counsel, so that when we need to go to someone, we know to whom to go.

Miss Alice knew something I did not know. That was why I watched for every chance to be with her, to observe her in action. . .[4]

Catherine Marshall, *Christy*

13

Rhythm: Work and Rest

Sustained and Productive

Year after year, nineteenth-century English novelist Anthony Trollope turned out novel after novel.[1] Trollope wrote over sixty books by keeping to a disciplined writing schedule that brought him to his desk every morning at 5:30 A.M. and that set his pen and notebook on his lap while riding the train to and from his full-time job at the postal service. So committed was Trollope to his "self-imposed laws" that he abided by them even on sea voyages in which he had to periodically leave his cabin table to be sick.

When I have commenced a new book, I have always
prepared a diary, divided into weeks, and carried on for the

*period which I have allowed myself for the completion of
the work. In this I have entered, day by day, the number
of pages I have written . . . There has ever been the record
before me, and a week passed with an insufficient number of
pages has been a blister to my eye, and a month so disgraced
would have been a sorrow to my heart.*[2]

Anthony Trollope, *An Autobiography*

When work is sustained, the mental "frequency" for
related thought stays tuned and ready to accept signals.
The sustained activity gathers momentum, producing
more thought, deeper discovery, a created object, or an
accomplished project.

In contrast, when work is intermittent, related thought
loses a connection that is difficult to resume. Like a seed
planted but not looked after, thought and work already
invested—however promising and wonderful—aren't given
the opportunity to yield any result. Progress is at risk whenever a schedule of sustained work is discarded for any
length of time.

I find that inattention to a project causes it to slip so far
back in my mind that it seems impossible to find it all again.
It's as if it slipped off an imaginary cranial back ledge. Can
I reach back in my mind far enough to find it? Will there
be time to pull all the pieces forward before I have to let it
go again? Will what I find be the same as I left it?

If the project is disregarded long enough, the memory
of its content gradually vanishes. What takes its place is
an alien voice telling me how impossible and ridiculous
my endeavor was in the first place. Without a mind full
of content, I find it difficult to battle that accusing voice.
The ignored project is then apt to be ignored even longer,
if not abandoned.

153

The focus of sustained work doesn't have to be a life-time research goal, or full-time job or calling, or yearlong creative endeavor. It may be a single project or problem or dream that you want to complete or solve or develop. The time frame may be a summer, a single week, or a three-month sabbatical. Or the project may simply need an uninterrupted weekend of sustained attention.

I had forgotten what fun it is to do nothing else but work on one definite subject, thinking about it and in terms of it all the time . . .[3]

Anne Morrow Lindbergh, *Hour of Gold, Hour of Lead*

Swimming Underwater

Distraction is the enemy of sustained productive work. Physical separation from distraction is the first line of defense, but the surest defense is a strong ability to concentrate. Without concentration, even a bare, soundless room can't guarantee one's mind stays focused on that work. In *Finding Flow*, University of Chicago professor of psychology Mihaly Csikszentmihalyi writes, "Without focus, consciousness is in a state of chaos . . . Unless one learns to concentrate, and is able to invest the effort, thoughts will scatter without reaching any conclusion."[4]

When thought is concentrated, you are in a position to become immersed in your project, to sink down into the deep richness of your mind. When so immersed, you are surrounded by only relevant thoughts. They push against you, waiting to be shaped by you. Nothing stands between

154

you and these thoughts, no distortion or interruption by anything external.

Here she could lie for half a day undistracted, holding pleasant and incomplete conceptions in her mind—almost in her hands.[5]

Willa Cather, *The Song of the Lark*

Imagine yourself swimming deep underwater in an outdoor pool on a warm summer day. Water covers your ears, your mouth, your fingertips. With muffled sound and limited visibility, you exist in a state disconnected from activity on the pool surface. Now imagine yourself swimming up from near the bottom. The deeper you are, the longer it takes to swim to the surface. Consider the moment of reaching the surface and the onslaught of sensory stimuli—the light; the feel of the air; the sounds of swimmers splashing, laughing, talking. An immersed state of mind is to swimming underwater as a nonimmersed state of mind is to being at the pool surface.

Immersion in your thoughts separates you from people and things around you. You are separated by dense and weighty, albeit ethereal, matter just as surely as an underwater and surface swimmer are separated by dense, heavy pool water. Yet the nature of sharing daily life with people and things requires that a significant amount of time be spent on the surface, and that time is often required intermittently and at a moment's notice. Periods of immersion, therefore, are often punctuated by the need to swim up from the deep mental waters back to the surface to participate in daily life. Then to dive back down again to continue work.

Anyhow this goes on all the morning: . . . I live entirely in [my brain], and come to the surface rather obscurely and am often unable to think what to say when we walk round the Square, which is bad I know. Perhaps it may be a good sign for the book though.[6]

Virginia Woolf, *A Writer's Diary*

Such a deep state of concentration as immersion is not needed for all of our mental assignments. But a great many do require this, or at least would benefit considerably from being worked out while in such a state. To give this degree of commitment, however, requires time and practice (immersion doesn't happen on command), and perhaps more significantly, a willingness to be summoned out of immersion, only to return to it again. And repeat as needed.

Saving the Best Strength

Marie and Pierre Curie began their married life devoted only to each other and to science. This choice affected everything about their lives. In her mother's biography, author Eve Curie describes her parents' tiny three-room flat:

Marie and Pierre had done nothing to decorate their three tiny rooms. They even refused the furniture offered them by Dr. Curie: every sofa and chair would be one more object to dust in the morning and to furbish up on days of full cleaning. Marie could not do it; she hadn't time. In any case what was the good of a sofa or chair, as the Curies had agreed to do away with meetings and calls? . . . At one end of the table was Marie's chair; at the other, Pierre's. On the table were treatises on physics, a petroleum lamp, a bunch of flowers; and that was all.[7]

Although this early singleness of purpose eventually expanded to include children and a comfortable home, it initially allowed Marie and Pierre to devote their time and energy to their laboratory work. This work led to Marie's receipt of the Nobel Prize in Physics in 1903 for the discovery of radioactivity, the first Nobel Prize ever awarded to a woman, and another in 1911 for the discovery of radium.

Granted, no matter how austere we make our homes or how many social obligations we decline, few of us will achieve an accomplishment for which we will win a Nobel Prize. Nevertheless, what each of us has to accomplish in our lives requires enormous physical and mental energy. And like Marie Curie, we may need to say no to a great many things so that we have the energy to do the work and think the thoughts needed in order to accomplish what has been given us to accomplish.

None of us is infinitely capable. There is a limit to the number of problems any of us can attempt to solve at any one time, the number of conversations we can replay, the depth of insights we can explore. Each of us has a finite number of brain cells that, as hard as we try to persuade them to do otherwise, can carry out only a finite number of cognitive processes before they scream for rest.

She had not yet conserved enough energy to resume thinking on a through-November basis.[8]

Joan Didion, *The Last Thing He Wanted*

If we squander our daily allotment of brain-cell activity on mind-numbing television, the portion we have to give to what we really should be doing is decreased. If we squander still more worrying about issues over which we have no control, the portion available for our true assignments decreases even more. If we jump to say yes to this activity and are bludgeoned by guilt when saying no to another, the allotment of brain-cell activity we have for our God-given assignments soon dwindles to little or nothing. We have soon given away our best strength.

What assignments has God given you? It may indeed be a pursuit that will win you a Nobel Prize. It may be to laugh and play with children. Your assignment may be to teach, or paint, or fly a plane. Are you reserving sufficient strength to meet this assignment? Where might your best strength be leaking out? Ralph Waldo Emerson said, "The crime which bankrupts men and states is job-work—declining from your main design, to serve a turn here or there."[9]

Picture yourself sitting at a table such as Marie and Pierre's. What can you add to the tabletop? Whom and what can you allow around the table? What must you keep from adjacent rooms? All the while keeping your best strength.

Beachcombing

Walking along a shoreline is a lovely way to spend an afternoon. The sound of water is meditative and mesmerizing as its waves roll and crash onto the shore, over and over, unleashing water to ripple across rocks or to be sucked into sand as it rushes backward. On the Florida shore, the air is warm and salty; on the Great Lakes in northern Minnesota, cool and pine-scented. The combination of sunshine and water softens my soul and mind like heat softens wax.

Relaxation is an inevitable outcome of such a leisurely activity. But when an opportunity to walk along a shore presents itself, I seek an additional outcome: the discovery of great rocks or shells. This is a task of pure pleasure and no pressure. I don't have to make the rocks or design the shells. I am not responsible for them in any way. I just get to find them.

And I have found many treasures: large egg-shaped pieces of granite; hard agates layered in shades of crimson; black, shiny lava; smooth, gray, flat rocks, polished thin enough to fit in the palm of a hand. Sand dollars the size of my thumbnail; periwinkles that burrow instantaneously back into the sand after each wave; one-shelled sea creatures nestled inside other one-shelled sea creatures.

> *The sound of the surf, the big washing machine of ocean, sometimes seems to rinse out my brain, or at any rate, it expands me and it slows me down.*[10]
>
> Anne Lamott, *Traveling Mercies*

An even greater treasure I've found while hunting rocks and shells is a treasure of thought. Engaged in this carefree task and calmed by the sensory pleasantries of rocks and shells and sights and smells, my mind begins to soar, expand, roll, do flips. I leave the shore with a fresh mind, new insights, and an eagerness to revisit some project.

In *Creativity*, Mihaly Csikszentmihalyi explains this mental phenomenon. When an activity requires some but not all of our attention, creative mental activity develops in the background. "Because these thoughts are not in the center of attention, they are left to develop on their own. There is no need to direct them, to criticize them prematurely, to make them do hard work. And of course it is just this freedom and playfulness that makes it possible for leisurely thinking to come up with original formulations and solutions."[11]

Other semiautomatic activities Csikszentmihalyi recommends: walking, driving, swimming, showering, gardening, weaving, carpentry. Add to this list cleaning, knitting, playing the piano, driving, or any other solitary activity that doesn't require hard thinking. Psychologist and author James Hillman lauds the fruitfulness of walking: "With the soul-calming language of walking, the dartings of the mind begin to form into a direction."[12]

This time of mental free play should not be sabotaged by forcing yourself to think about something. But it may be helpful to plant a hint in your mind of what it may want to tinker with while you are otherwise occupied. Or plan a time of concentrated thought on this subject before your walk or other semiautomatic activity. Then after you've released your mind to soar for a while, meet yourself with pen and paper and mine your thoughts.

In *If You Want to Write*, Brenda Ueland assures us of the benefits of such creative idleness.

> If it is the dreamy idleness that children have, an idleness when you walk alone for a long, long time, or take a long, dreamy time at dressing, or lie in bed at night and thoughts come and go, or dig in a garden, or drive a car for many hours alone, or play the piano, or sew, or paint ALONE . . . that is creative idleness. With all my heart I tell you and reassure you: at such times you are being slowly filled and re-charged with warm imagination, with wonderful, living thoughts.[13]

Rejuvenation

"Man, have you got a tight scalp. That's tension. You prob'ly use your brain all th' time. That's what does it. Some people, their scalp just rolls around on their head like baggy pantyhose."[14]

Jan Karon, *A Light in the Window*

Right before a vacation, my mental stress seems to peak. I can hardly concentrate or generate ideas. It is hard to think a thought through to completion. I want to leave my mind's contents on my desk alongside my papers. I long to lie on a beach with an empty mind, using it only to read the novels packed in my bag.

Once en route, I want to escape immediately to vacation mind-set. I try hard not to think about anything required of me. This attitude prevails for some time into the vacation. Then, slowly, almost imperceptibly, my mind is piqued by some remembrance of a project, goal, or interest. I may even visit a bookstore and come away not with an escapist paperback but a serious book about that project, goal, or interest. Eventually I take out my notebook and write down an idea. *I'll do such and so when I get back,* I think. I get excited.

This pattern of revival is confirmed by Anne Morrow Lindbergh in *Gift from the Sea:* "At first, the tired body takes over completely. As on shipboard, one descends into a deck-chair apathy . . . And then, some morning in the second week, the mind wakes, comes to life again. Not in a city sense—no—but beach-wise. It begins to drift, to play, to turn over in gentle careless rolls like those lazy waves on the beach."[15]

161

What accounts for the transformation from a prevacation, squeezed-shut mind to a mind open like a sponge? Quite simply, a true and solid break (as opposed to a break of the sort that can be as full of requirement, action, and chaos as any other day). A solid break is a time in which the mind can empty itself of overused and boring thoughts. A time in which the superfluous can boil off, leaving a rich core concentrate. During a solid break, the tedium can be forgotten and mental ruts washed smooth. The original passion of projects and goals can refuel the energy that the extensive "to-do lists" associated with them have spent. During a solid break, you can take back your mind to do with as you please. You can use it yourself or just let it exist. Let it lie with you on a beach chair. Let it move only when it's ready.

Without downtime, the mind becomes as ineffective as a muscle that is continually contracted or a sponge that is never squeezed out. Solid breaks of one, two, or more weeks probably provide maximum recovery time, but shorter breaks and daily downtimes, in the form of relaxation and an adequate night's sleep, are also valuable and critical.

> *I looked at my watch. Nine fifty-four. Time to go home and get your slippers on and . . . to sit with your feet up and think of nothing. Time to start yawning over your magazine. Time to be a human being, a householder, a man with nothing to do but rest and suck in the night air and rebuild the brain for tomorrow.*[16]
>
> Raymond Chandler, *The Lady in the Lake*

Shockingly, a weekly day of rest has the same stature within the Ten Commandments as the admonition against murder. "Six days you shall labor and do all your work, but the seventh day is a Sabbath, to the LORD your God. On it you shall not do any work . . ."[17] A weekly day of rest, in full knowledge of bills to be paid and work on the desk, of towels to be washed and groceries to be bought. A weekly day of rest taken freely, proactively, worshipfully, without guilt. Rejuvenation as commandment, not luxury.

14

ACTION

Knowledge Lived

Acquiring knowledge in everyday life is not an intellectual exercise. The goal is not knowledge but to live knowledgeably. What we know should affect what we do.

> So things go on as before with those who think a great deal and effect nothing, and those who think nothing evidently doing it all.[1]
>
> Saul Bellow, *Herzog*

Knowledge ignored becomes useless. For example, it would be foolish to begin a road trip and pass the last gas station in town knowing that my tank is nearly empty. Stalled by the side of the road forty miles out of town, I would be without excuse for my predicament.

Each of us could probably list at least five predicaments we might have avoided during the last year if we had only acted on what we knew. Perhaps a predicament arising from not acting on what was known about one's child or about the industry in which one worked, or not following a physician's instruction or considering the counsel of a wise friend. Or not acting on what we knew to be right.

He drove unsteadily down the road, his eyes blurred with nausea. O God, he thought, the decisions you force on people, suddenly, with no time to consider . . . The trouble is, he thought, we know the answers—we Catholics are damned by our knowledge. There's no need for me to work anything out—there is only one answer: to kneel down in the confessional and say . . .[2]

Graham Greene, *The Heart of the Matter*

Consider the amount of knowledge that God has made available about himself. A legitimate question to ask oneself: Has a reasonable amount of personal action resulted from that knowledge? Similarly, is there a direct relationship between that knowledge and my actions? As my knowledge has grown, have I acted on it in increasingly significant and mature ways?

The Book of Luke tells the story of a legal expert who tested Jesus with the question, "What must I do to inherit eternal life?"

Jesus replied with his own questions: "What is written in the Law? How do you read it?"

The legal expert responded, "Love the Lord your God with all your heart and with all your soul and with all your strength and with all your mind . . . Love your neighbor as yourself."[3]

Jesus affirmed the answer yet challenged the expert: You're right. Now go do it.

Each of us, to a large extent, is prepared to go and do. All the living, reading, learning, working, traveling, and caring for friends and family that we have done has already filled each of us with a rich marinated mix of knowledge to be put on the table of life. Use it freely. Picture it freely flowing from your mind infusing all your actions. Enriching your life. Giving your life integrity. Equipping your life to be used in service for the lives of others and for God.

Prepare your minds for action.[4]

From the Book of 1 Peter

Not all knowledge can and should be put into play right away. But when knowledge is stored, it should be with an eye toward eventual use. An opportunity for its use may come gradually over time as new knowledge coalesces with old knowledge, ultimately becoming a springboard for action. Or an opportunity may be sudden and specific, when in a Queen Esther–type moment you'll see that you know something "for such a time as this."[5] In both cases, acting on what you know allows you to use all that has gone before you in life to positively and responsibly shape what is here and now and what is to come.

To Choose the Way

Three millennia ago, King Solomon wrote, "The wisdom of the prudent is to give thought to their ways."[6] Choosing the way—moment by moment—is how we ultimately direct our lives. To give thought to one's choices and ways is to stake a claim on one's life.

> *It had been a long lesson but she had learned it. Either you think—or else others have to think for you and take power from you . . .*[7]
>
> F. Scott Fitzgerald, *Tender Is the Night*

If we don't give thought to our choices and ways, we lose the distinctiveness of our lives; we become generic, controlled by circumstances, myths, false predictions, unsound advice, routine, and mood; we make it easy for other people to live our lives for us.

If we don't give thought to our choices and ways, we fail to recognize the additive and directional force that daily decisions exert on our lives. We fail to make conscious choices that maintain a consistent positive momentum.

If we don't give thought to our choices and ways, we may be passively set on a course with a trajectory that will take us light-years from the course on which active thought would have set us. Such an alteration in life course may be impossible to correct, even if the lack of thought is quickly corrected.

If we don't give thought to our choices and ways, we fail to shape the rough materials of our lives into the final product intended by the Creator.

If we don't give thought to our choices and ways, issues propagate, becoming more difficult to approach than they were in their virgin state before the results of nonthinking made them worse.

I knew we were on a dangerous ride, but I still didn't want to end it even if I had known how. It was too much of a good thing, a heedless, continuous, romping jig and party—when I could keep from thinking. Not thinking, refusing to think, got to be a steady habit for me.[8]

Kent Haruf, *The Tie That Binds*

Choose your way with thought, moment by moment. Anticipate what's coming, observe what's happening around you, watch for markers, heed intuitive red flags, recognize cause and effect, avoid raw trial and error.

The prophet Jeremiah relays this message from the Lord: "Stand at the crossroads and look; ask for the ancient paths, ask where the good way is, and walk in it, and you will find rest for your souls."[9]

This ancient message remains valuable today. Stand at the crossroads and look. Think. Multiple roads begin from the same point, but each takes you by longer and longer increments a great distance from where you started and from where you'd be if you had chosen another road. Stand and look and think. Where does each road go? Follow it through with your mind.

Paths can be difficult to extrapolate into the future; it can be easier when you can see patterns of paths that have already been followed. Read of the ancient paths taken by Moses, Samuel, Joseph, Esther, and others, and those recommended by the sacred authors of Psalms, Proverbs, and Ecclesiastes. Note the differences between the successful ancient paths and the detours that led to ruin. Read biographies of great men and women. Note their choices, their successes and failures.

Think it through. Choose your way with care.

Contributions of Excellence

A visit to Washington, D.C., brought me to the National Archives. Like much of what I saw in our nation's capital—from the tangible beauty of the architecture to the conceptual beauty of our republic—what I saw in the Archives reflected genius and contributions of excellence.

The Archives displayed examples of the real-life work of important Americans. Of a Civil War nurse: the daily notes of Clara Barton, the founder of the American Red Cross. Of an inventor: the journal of Alexander Graham Bell, recording the day his telephone finally worked. Of a minister: Martin Luther King Jr.'s personal typed copy of "I Have a Dream." Of presidents: the handwritten notes of President Jimmy Carter, in which he worked out the Camp David Peace Accords; a draft of President Dwight Eisenhower's D-Day speech; and notes of President George Bush Sr.'s Desert Storm speech.

Those who viewed these displays around me were contributors of excellence in their own right. Mothers and fathers raising their children well. Teachers going out of their way to gather knowledge and return it to the classroom. Students wanting to learn more and doing so on their own. Men and women, active in their communities, leading and serving. Artists supplying beauty of sound and sight. Pastors and priests, grocers, marketing experts, hairdressers, waiters and waitresses, realtors, bankers, pharmacists.

When she was young, she'd dreamed of being a nurse and setting up a kind of Hull House for the sick and poor—a quixotic dream about climbing to the highest pinnacle of herself where the air was clear and bracing and she trembled with purpose.[10]

Faith Sullivan, *The Empress of One*

In and around the Archives, still more contributors of excellence were evident. The tradesmen who built and furnished the Archives and other stately buildings that line the streets of Washington, D.C. The archivists who catalog and protect the historical documents of our country. The law enforcement officers who keep people and things protected. The administrators who manage these great institutions. The cooks who make the food that will be served in the restaurants down the street. The road workers and air traffic controllers who make the way to the Archives smooth and safe.

Our society is the beneficiary of a multitude of contributions of excellence, which have been made possible by applied minds as well as applied hearts and hands. Among these contributions, past and present, countless works are represented and infinite callings fulfilled, gifts consummated, needs met, and lives lifted.

Mary Lyon, who had found intellectual and emotional stimulus from the church at Baptist Corner, kindled at the possibility of dedicating her life to the service of God in a way that made continuing demands on her power to learn and to reflect, as well as on her eagerness to serve.[11]

Elizabeth Alden Green, *Mary Lyon and Mount Holyoke*

Pondering the huge potential each of us has to make our society better, to satisfy deep needs in our communities, and to be used by God is enough to make one's soul ache with longing to find the place where one can contribute gifts of excellence. Or to make one's soul dance with joy at the gracious fortune to have already found such a place.

A Link in the Chain

I am grateful when people mark their paths—for example, in personal conversation, books, or lectures—so that someone wishing or needing to follow a similar path can better find the way. It is a gift when someone passes on what they've discovered, warns us how to avoid the mistakes they made, or shows us how to benefit from their successes. With such a gift, there is no hoarding of success or knowledge.

My own recovery, I realize, was greatly furthered by the love, understanding, and support of those around me. But I was also indebted to many unknown friends who had gone before me and left their testimony to illumine the shadowy path. In return I leave my own record, bearing witness to my journey, for others who may follow.[12]

Anne Morrow Lindbergh, *Hour of Gold, Hour of Lead*

Sharing what you know requires that you let what you know come out. Your knowledge is like the sap in a tree, derived from the nourishment of your experiences, tastes, and opportunities for knowledge. But like a tree's sap, your knowledge is contained. Unless you open your mouth, use your pen, or act, what you know remains hidden.

Some knowledge must be received and passed on in pure form, as if cradling a fragile vase passed from grandmother

171

to granddaughter. Yet other knowledge can be offered as a base on which to build. For example, great discoveries in the scientific world are made when the work of one scientist is published, and another scientist takes it a step further, and another a step further. But scientists aren't the only ones to add their knowledge to the knowledge of others. In any good discussion, two or more people put their knowledge on the table and build something sturdier and taller than any of them had on their own.

Receiving knowledge from and passing it on to others, building on it as we can, places us as links in the chain of knowledge and discovery that spans generations. Maybe we will never know what our link in a chain has been, but how we each should hope to have some link.

Find a way to be a link in the chain, to make what you've learned available to someone else. What can you pass on? What forward movement in another person can your words set in motion? What push can you give that sets someone's swing soaring? Talk, show, write, and live so that what is in you finds a way to come out and be given away.

15

THE CONCLUSION
OF THE MATTER

The Pursuit of Wisdom

Israel's King Solomon has been regarded as the wisest person who ever lived. The Old Testament reports that God gave Solomon wisdom, insight, and understanding "as measureless as the sand on the seashore,"[1] and that "the whole world sought audience with Solomon to hear the wisdom God had put in his heart."[2]

Solomon details his exploration of wisdom in the Book of Ecclesiastes. In this book, the wisest man of all writes these surprising words: "When I applied myself to know wisdom . . . *then I saw all that God has done"* (emphasis added).[3]

Solomon's words make me want to reach back through the ages, tap him on the shoulder, and ask, "Was your effort to know wisdom successful or not?" After all, he doesn't *exactly* say he found wisdom through his applied effort, but only that his eyes were opened to all God had done. Yet Solomon, more than a bit wiser than me, apparently believed his effort successful.

Awe of God appears to be a necessary subdestination on the journey to true wisdom. Solomon came to recognize that finding true wisdom necessitates comprehending the incomprehensibleness of God. "No one can comprehend what goes on under the sun. Despite all his efforts to search it out, man cannot discover its meaning."[4] These words echo the dialogue between Job and God in which God fired the questions, Do *you* know. . . ? Do *you* watch . . . ? Can *you* . . . ? Will *you* . . . ? Job answers: No. No. No. No.

I ended my first book with the words no answer. I know now, Lord, why you utter no answer. You are yourself the answer. Before your face questions die away. What other answer would suffice?[5]

C. S. Lewis, Till We Have Faces

Each of us is called to the same task as Solomon: to apply our minds to know wisdom. Is the end to which we are being led also the same? Is simple and profound awe of God the final and ultimate universal outcome of a fully applied mind? Awe is an abstract concept, however, more a state of being. Yet when we speak of a person having wisdom, we regard that person as having a practical attribute—one that allows her to judge accurately; to discern between right and wrong and between good, better, and best; and to have deep knowledge and understanding of the important matters of life. Simply put, a wise person generally knows what to do and what is important. So what is the relationship between abstract awe and practical concrete wisdom?

Solomon offers a clue. Based on his search to know wisdom and the resulting insight as to the awesomeness of God, he writes, "Here is the conclusion of the matter: Fear God and keep his commandments, for this is the whole duty of man."[6]

The link, therefore, between abstract awe and practical concrete wisdom appears to be that a fully applied mind takes us to a point of being awed by God. And the practical outcome of that awe is respect for God in all that we do, which includes keeping his laws. In other words—wisdom.

Stand in awe of God.[7]

From the Book of Ecclesiastes

If Solomon had never applied his mind, he wouldn't have seen all that God had done. Without seeing, there would have been no awe. Without awe, no concluding respect of God and commitment to his commandments. No wisdom. Likewise for us: First we apply our minds; then we see; then we are awed; then we respect; then we obey. Then we know wisdom.

Reunion

The story is familiar. Adam and Eve are in the garden, luxuriating in beauty, leisure, and companionship. God places only one limitation on their freedom: They are not to eat from the tree of knowledge of good and evil. Yet Eve believes the guile of the serpent who tempts her to eat the forbidden fruit. Adam follows. Aware of their transgression, God quickly terminates their stay in paradise and ushers them into what we know as the real world, complete with pain in childbirth and the toil associated with work.

The question that rings in my head when I hear this story is, What is wrong with the knowledge of good and evil? After all, isn't this one of the highest types of knowledge we can seek? Haven't volumes been written on this? Don't we teach our children the difference between right and wrong? Aren't our laws themselves based on an interpretation of good and evil? In fact, how can we be holy without knowing good from evil?

Why did reaching for the fruit of this knowledge earn Adam and Eve's eviction? If God simply wanted to test their obedience, why didn't he instead forbid the fruit from some other tree?

I'm not sure of the theologically correct answer to these questions, but this is what I wonder: Perhaps because God himself was holy (completely pure and blameless), he simply desperately wanted the free-willed people he had created to be holy also. And as long as they didn't experience evil, they would stay holy. As a parent, I can imagine that God also wanted to shield them from even knowing that evil existed, to shield them from the fact that there could be anything contrary to their present joy and security. Consider that deep well of love and dread from which we firmly, but delicately, warn our children: "Don't talk to strangers." Maybe it was from such a well that God himself warned about the knowledge of evil, and consequently, its mirror image, good: "Don't eat!"

But they did eat, and in so doing Adam and Eve discovered evil, because disobeying God—acting contrary to the holy God—was to know evil, as one who had done evil. They had known the highest good—friendship and companionship with God in a perfect world—and now they knew evil.

God and his people were now at an impasse. With God being absolutely holy, anything contrary to holiness could not coexist with him. So away from him they had to go.

Yet God loved his people, whom he had made.

The rest of the Bible is the story of God resolving this impasse. It is the story of God finding a way for each of us to be holy—when it is obvious that none of us is so on our own—so that he and his people could have each other back. His greatest and final act of offering us holiness was through the sacrifice of his son, Jesus Christ. In that sacrifice, the knowledge of good and evil came full circle. Holy God himself took on all the evil in all the world. He substituted his good for our evil so that the people he created and loved could start fresh with his holiness.

We have been made holy through the sacrifice of the body of Jesus Christ once for all.[8]

From the Book of Hebrews

Now what does this have to do with thinking?

First, although it is through Jesus Christ that we have the opportunity to be made holy, we need to use our minds to pursue this and think about this. We are not passively led to accept this offer. Neither is the offer forced upon us against our will. Because we choose to accept or reject it, we must set our minds on considering the offer.

Second, if we choose to accept the offer, to take Christ at his word and agree to exchange our evil—that is, contrariness to God—for his holiness, we become holy in his sight. Once granted holiness, we would be wise not to mock this undeserved exchange by choosing to continue in ways that are contrary to God. Therefore, we must set about knowing the ways of God, the ways that are pleasing and acceptable to him. And the only way to know the ways of God is by studying Scripture. We may think we can intuit the ways of God, but as Adam and Eve learned, it is best not to assume we can make these distinctions on our own. After all, consider Christ himself, who used Scripture to battle successive temptations to choose a way contrary to God.

> *As soon as [Alyosha] reflected seriously he was convinced of the existence of God and immortality, and at once he instinctively said to himself: "I want to live for immortality, and I will accept no compromise."*[9]
>
> Fyodor Dostoevsky, *Brothers Karamazov*

Reunion with God is gained by starting over with Christ's holiness, and it is lived out by going to God as the provider of the knowledge of his ways, the only true rule for good and evil. Think about the offer; learn his ways.

Thinking with Your Face toward the Light

Wisdom and knowledge began before me, my parents and grandparents, the American founding fathers, Aristotle,

Plato, Socrates, Solomon, Moses, and Abraham. Wisdom and knowledge existed before the creation of the world. Before anything, wisdom and knowledge were. Embodied in God.

Who has understood the mind of the LORD,

or instructed him as his counselor?

Whom did the LORD consult to enlighten him,

and who taught him the right way?

Who was it that taught him knowledge

or showed him the path of understanding?[10]

From the Book of Isaiah

Of his studies prior to his conversion to Christianity, Saint Augustine wrote in *The Confessions,* "What profit was it to me that I . . . read and understood by myself as many books as I could get concerning the so-called liberal arts? I enjoyed these, not recognizing the source of whatever elements of truth and certainty they contained. I had turned my back to the light and my face to the things it illuminated, and so no light played upon my own face, or on the eyes that perceived them."[11]

To think with your face toward the light, as Augustine later learned, is to learn and think in the direction of God. It is to recognize God as the original source of wisdom and knowledge. It is to go about all you do, all you learn, all you puzzle over, positioned with your attention toward God and enlightened by the knowledge and wisdom of God. It is to see the thread of God in everything, to be aware that "the whole earth is full of his glory."[12]

They seemed to be staring at the dark, but their eyes were watching God.[13]

Zora Neale Hurston, *Their Eyes Were Watching God*

With your face and mind turned toward God, you see that children and playgrounds and schools and doctors' offices and grocery stores and boardrooms and freeway entrance ramps are full of his glory. Courses you take and books you read, regardless of the presence of a religious key word in the title, point to and glorify God. You recognize a painting's resonance with ultimate truth, whether or not it contains a Madonna or crucified Christ. You may study mathematics or music for years without hearing the name of God invoked, but you don't miss the testimony of the divine elegance and beauty found in both. Science may appear to speak of only godless hypotheses and lifeless statistics, but the principles it adheres to and uncovers shout the logic and order that underlie nature. God's creativity is evident to you in all creating—whether sculpture, literature, homes, computers, pharmaceuticals, or pies.

The source of all wisdom and knowledge—God—illuminates the mind of one whose face is turned toward him.

Glory be to God.

NOTES

Introduction

1. F. Scott Fitzgerald, *Tender Is the Night* (New York: Scribner's, 1962), 94.

2. H. A. Overstreet, *The Mature Mind* (New York: W. W. Norton, 1949), 284.

3. Faith Sullivan, *The Cape Ann* (New York: Penguin, 1988), 120.

Chapter 1: A Mind for Life

1. Mark 12:28–30.

2. David Coomes, *Dorothy L. Sayers: A Careless Rage for Life* (Batavia, Ill.: Lion, 1992), 205–6.

3. 1 Cor. 2:16.

4. Jonathan Edwards, *The Importance and Advantage of a Thorough Knowledge of Divine Truth* (n.d.), Christian Classics Ethereal Library, http://www.ccel.org/e/edwards/sermons/divineTruth.html (6 October 2002).

5. Elizabeth Alden Green, *Mary Lyon and Mount Holyoke* (Hanover, N.H.: University Press of New England, 1979), 26.

6. Heb. 3:1.

7. Thomas R. Kelly, *A Testament of Devotion* (San Francisco: HarperSanFrancisco, 1992), 9.

8. Ron Hansen, *Mariette in Ecstasy* (New York: HarperPerennial, 1992), 41.

9. Philip B. Kunhardt Jr., Philip B. Kunhardt III, and Peter W. Kunhardt, *Lincoln: An Illustrated Biography* (New York: Alfred A. Knopf, 1992), 399.

10. Ps. 139:14.

11. Carolyn Keene, *The Mystery of the 99 Steps* (New York: Grosset & Dunlap, 1966), 72.

12. Kaye Gibbons, *A Virtuous Woman* (New York: Vintage, 1990), 25.

13. George Eliot, *Middlemarch* (Boston: Houghton Mifflin, 1968), 473.

14. Blaise Pascal, *The Mind on Fire*, ed. James M. Houston (London: Hodder & Stoughton, 1989), 82.

15. Annie Dillard, *The Writing Life* (New York: HarperPerennial, 1989), 78–79.

16. Saul Bellow, *Herzog* (New York: Viking, 1964), 104–5.

17. Matt. 25:14–30.

18. Henry David Thoreau, *The Heart of Thoreau's Journals*, ed. Odell Shepard (New York: Dover, 1961), 213.

19. Catherine Marshall, *Christy* (New York: Spire, 1968), 68.

Chapter 2: The Needed Balance

1. Pope John Paul II, *Fides Et Ratio* (1998), Vatican: The Holy Father, http://www.vatican.va/holy_father/john_paul_ii/encyclicals (7 October 2002).

2. Luke 2:19.

3. Jer. 51:15.

4. Jer. 31:3.

5. Luke 13:34.

6. Matt. 10:16.

7. Martin Luther King Jr., *Strength to Love* (New York: Harper & Row, 1963), 5.

8. Nathaniel Hawthorne, "Ethan Brand," in *Tales and Sketches* (New York: Library of America, 1982), 1051–67.

9. Ibid., 1055.

10. Ibid., 1056–57.

11. Ibid., 1064.

12. Ibid.

Chapter 3: Forward Movement

1. C. S. Lewis, *Perelandra* (New York: Macmillan, 1965), 60.

2. Daphne du Maurier, *Jamaica Inn* (Garden City, N.Y.: Doubleday, 1936), 133.

3. Betty Smith, *A Tree Grows in Brooklyn* (New York: Harper & Bros., 1943), 227.

4. Oswald Chambers, *My Utmost for His Highest* (Westwood, N.J.: Barbour, 1963), 62.

5. Charles Williams, *The Place of the Lion* (Grand Rapids: Eerdmans, 1991), 9.

6. Sue Grafton, *"O" Is for Outlaw* (New York: Henry Holt & Co., 1999), 28.

7. Joan Didion, *The Last Thing He Wanted* (New York: Alfred A. Knopf, 1996), 79.

8. Pam Belluck, "Nuns Offer Clues to Alzheimer's and Aging," *The New York Times* (7 May 2001). www.nytimes.com/2001/05/07/health/07NUNS.html (29 June 2003).

9. D. A. Snowdon, L. H. Greiner, and W. R. Markesbery, "Linguistic Ability in Early Life and the Neuropathy of Alzheimer's Disease and Cerebrovascular Disease: Findings from the Nun Study." *Annals of the New York Academy of Science* 903(2000): 34–38.

10. Isa. 40:21.

11. Matt. 16:9.

12. Sue Grafton, *"M" is for Malice* (New York: Fawcett Crest, 1998), 23.

13. Edwards, *Importance and Advantage of a Thorough Knowledge*.

14. Herman Melville, *Moby Dick*, in *Moby Dick/Billy Budd* (London: Octopus, 1984), 48.

Chapter 4: Breadth of Life, Fullness of Thought

1. Phil. 4:8.

2. P. D. James, *The Skull Beneath the Skin* (New York: Warner, 1996), 298.

3. *Classification Outline*, Library of Congress, 2002, http://ww.lcweb.loc.gov/catdir/cpso/lcco/lcco.html (16 July 2002).

4. T. H. White, *The Once and Future King* (New York: G. P. Putnam's Sons, 1958), 174.

5. Mortimer J. Adler, ed., "Syntopicon," *Great Books of the Western World*, vols. 1 and 2 (Chicago: Encyclopaedia Britannica, Inc., 1952).

6. Thornton Wilder, *Our Town* (New York: Perennial Classics, 1998), 46.

7. John Locke, *Locke: Selections*, ed. Sterling P. Lamprecht (New York: Scribner's, 1956), 23–24.

8. Terry Tempest Williams, *An Unspoken Hunger* (New York: Pantheon, 1994), 3.

9. Henry Adams, *The Education of Henry Adams*, vol. 1 (New York: Time Reading Program, 1964), 2.

10. Willa Cather, *The Song of the Lark* (New York: Penguin, 1999), 298.

11. Zora Neale Hurston, *Their Eyes Were Watching God* (New York: Perennial Library, 1990), 183.

12. Prov. 27:17.

13. Eleanor Roosevelt, *You Learn by Living* (New York: Harper & Bros., 1960), 9.

14. Flannery O'Connor, *The Habit of Being*, ed. Sally Fitzgerald (New York: Vintage, 1979), 103.

15. Anne Morrow Lindbergh, *The Flower and the Nettle* (New York: Harcourt Brace Jovanovich, 1976), 59.

16. Humphrey Carpenter, *The Inklings* (Boston: Houghton Mifflin, 1979), 117.

17. William Maxwell, *Time Will Darken It* (Boston: Nonpareil, 1987), 81.

18. O'Connor, *The Habit of Being*, 103.

19. Ezek. 40:4.

20. Ralph Waldo Emerson, "The American Scholar," in *The Complete Essays and Other Writings of Ralph Waldo Emerson,* ed. Brooks Atkinson (New York: Random House, 1950), 47.

21. Ps. 19:1–2.

22. Mark 13:28.

23. Jane Austen, *Persuasion* (New York: Quality Paperback Book Club, 1996), 137.

24. "R. R. Bowker Releases U.S. Book Production Statistics, Showing Double-Digit Increase in 2001," R. R. Bowker LLC press release, April 2002, http://www.bowker.com/bowkerweb/Press_Releases/Stats_Story_on_Wire.htm (14 November 2002).

25. Virginia Woolf, *Granite & Rainbow* (New York: Harvest, 1975), 94.

26. Dorothy L. Sayers, *The Unpleasantness at the Bellona Club*, in *Clouds of Witnesses and The Unpleasantness at the Bellona Club* (New York: Harper & Row, 1956), 371.

Chapter 5: Accommodations for Thought

1. Dodie Smith, *I Capture the Castle* (New York: Wyatt, 1998), 3.

2. Ernest Dimnet, *The Art of Thinking* (New York: Simon & Schuster, 1930), 92.

3. Julia Cameron, *The Right to Write* (New York: Putnam, 1998), 193, 209–10.

4. Betty Smith, *A Tree Grows in Brooklyn*, 16.

5. Anne Morrow Lindbergh, *Hour of Gold, Hour of Lead* (New York: Harcourt Brace Jovanovich, 1973), 149.

6. Daphne du Maurier, *Myself When Young: The Shaping of a Writer* (Garden City, N.Y.: Doubleday, 1977), 168.

7. Austen, *Persuasion*, 72.

8. Num. 21: 8–9.

9. Graham Greene, *The Honorary Consul* (New York: Simon & Schuster, 1973), 287.

10. Barbara Kingsolver, *The Poisonwood Bible* (New York: HarperFlamingo, 1998), 56.

11. Virginia Woolf, *A Room of One's Own* (London: Harcourt Brace Jovanovich, 1989), 76.

12. Eve Curie, *Madame Curie* (Garden City, N.Y.: Garden City Publishing, 1940), 53.

13. Ibid., 107–10.

14. Dodie Smith, *I Capture the Castle*, 25.

15. Cather, *Song of the Lark*, 52.
16. Eccles. 3:1.
17. Virginia Woolf, *A Writer's Diary*, ed. Leonard Woolf (San Diego: Harcourt Brace, 1982), 50.

Chapter 6: Mental Readiness

1. Dodie Smith, *I Capture the Castle*, 301.
2. John Locke, *An Essay Concerning Human Understanding*, ed. Maurice Cranston (New York: Collier, 1965), 95.
3. Dan. 10:12.
4. Louise Fitzhugh, *Harriet the Spy* (New York: Harper & Row, 1964), 45.
5. Anne Lamott, *Bird by Bird* (New York: Anchor Books, 1995), 136.
6. Ibid., 133–44.
7. Grafton, *"O" Is for Outlaw*, 124.
8. Dimnet, *Art of Thinking*, 166.
9. William Gibson, *The Miracle Worker* (New York: Bantam, 1975), 30.
10. C. S. Lewis, *Till We Have Faces* (New York: Harcourt Brace, 1956), 294.
11. *Webster's New Dictionary of Synonyms* (Springfield, Mass.: G. & C. Merriam, 1978), 4a.
12. Lyrics, *Sarum Primer*, 1545.
13. Matt. 6:33.
14. Faith Sullivan, *The Empress of One* (Minneapolis: Milkwood Editions, 1996), 140.
15. G. K. Chesterton, "The Tremendous Adventure of Major Brown," in *Thirteen Detectives*, ed. Marie Smith (New York: Dodd, Mead & Company, 1987), 42.

Chapter 7: Befogged

1. Charles Williams, *War in Heaven* (Grand Rapids: Eerdmans, 1994), 248.
2. *Webster's New Dictionary of Synonyms*, 533.
3. Gustave Flaubert, *Madame Bovary* (New York: The Modern Library, 1957), 114.
4. Ps. 77:2–4.
5. Ps. 77:11–12.
6. Lam. 3:20–26.
7. John 14:27.
8. Graham Greene, *The Heart of the Matter* (New York: Penguin, 1999), 48.
9. Fitzgerald, *Tender Is the Night*, 93–94.
10. Georges Bernanos, *The Diary of a Country Priest*, trans. Pamela Morris (London: Fount, 1977), 1.

11. Flannery O'Connor, "The Geranium," in *The Complete Stories* (New York: Farrar, Straus & Giroux, 1999), 3.

12. du Maurier, *Jamaica Inn*, 25.

13. Charlotte Brontë, *Jane Eyre* (New York: Signet Classic, 1997), 322–23.

14. Fitzgerald, *Tender Is the Night*, 157.

Chapter 8: Self-Knowledge

1. Anna Quindlen, *Black and Blue* (New York: Random House, 1998), 54.

2. John W. Gardner, *Self-Renewal* (New York: Harper & Row, 1964), 13.

3. Isabel Briggs Myers, *Introduction to Type* (Palo Alto, Calif.: Consulting Psychologists Press, 1989).

4. Joanna Field, *A Life of One's Own* (Los Angeles: J. P. Tarcher, 1981), 12.

5. Sue Miller, *While I Was Gone* (New York: Ballantine, 1999), 261.

6. Anne Morrow Lindbergh, *Bring Me a Unicorn* (New York: Harcourt Brace Jovanovich, 1971), 104.

7. Graham Greene, *Our Man in Havana* (New York: Penguin, 1971), 67.

8. Elizabeth Pennisi, "The Human Genome," *Science*, 16 February 2001, 1177–80; and Carina Dennis, ed., "The Human Genome," *Nature*, 18 February 2001, 813–958.

9. Fitzhugh, *Harriet the Spy*, 240.

10. White, *Once and Future King*, 215.

Chapter 9: Truth

1. Williams, *Place of the Lion*, 136.

2. Daphne du Maurier, *Rebecca* (New York: Doubleday, 1965), 273–74.

3. O'Connor, *Habit of Being*, 100.

4. Virginia Woolf, *To the Lighthouse* (Hertfordshire: Wordsworth Classics, 1994), 34.

5. Lewis, *Perelandra*, 94.

6. Deut. 4:2.

7. Austen, *Persuasion*, 211.

8. C. S. Lewis, *That Hideous Strength* (New York: Collier Books, 1965), 234.

9. Kelly, *Testament of Devotion*, 10.

10. C. S. Lewis, *The Lion, the Witch, and the Wardrobe* (New York: Collier, 1970), 159.

11. Jer. 31:3.

12. Isa. 40:25.

Chapter 10: Questions and Answers

1. Graham Greene, *The Power and the Glory* (New York: Viking Press, 1968), 43.

2. Matt. 22:29.

3. Matt. 16:15.

4. Matt. 16:26.

5. Matt. 20:32.

6. Matt. 22:42.

7. Matt. 23:19.

8. Maxwell, *Time Will Darken It*, 86.

9. Matt. 21:23–27.

10. C. S. Lewis, *Surprised by Joy* (New York: Harcourt, Brace & World, 1955).

11. Chesterton, "The White Pillars Murder," in *Thirteen Detectives*, 19.

12. C. S. Lewis, *Out of the Silent Planet* (New York: Scribner, 1996), 41–42.

13. Leona Rostenberg and Madeleine Stern, *Old Books, Rare Friends* (New York: Doubleday, 1997), 171–76.

14. Prov. 24:3–4.

15. John W. Henderson, "The Yellow Brick Road to Penicillin: A Story of Serendipity," *Mayo Clinic Proceedings* 72, no. 7 (1997): 683–87.

16. Greene, *Our Man in Havana*, 71.

17. Keene, *Mystery of the 99 Steps*, 80.

18. Ps. 119:130.

19. Gen. 1:2.

20. Woolf, *A Room of One's Own*, 5.

21. Dorothy L. Sayers, *Whose Body?* (New York: Avon, 1961), 127.

22. Grafton, *"M" Is for Malice*, 228.

Chapter 11: Stretch and Strain

1. Lewis, *Till We Have Faces*, 249.

2. Hurston, *Their Eyes Were Watching God*, 20.

3. Jamie Langston Turner, *Some Wildflower in My Heart* (Minneapolis: Bethany House, 1998), 197–98.

4. John Dewey, *How We Think* (Boston: D. C. Heath, 1910), 13.

5. Tracy Kidder, "The Good Doctor," *New Yorker*, 10 July 2000, 40–57.

6. Greene, *Heart of the Matter*, 79.

7. James, *Skull Beneath the Skin*, 247.

8. 1 Sam. 13:14.

9. Fyodor Dostoevsky, *Brothers Karamazov*, trans. Constance Garnett (New York: Barnes & Noble Books, 1995), 156.

Chapter 12: Lifelong Learning

1. Billie Letts, *Where the Heart Is* (New York: Warner Books, 1998), 170.

2. Mortimer Adler, "Why Only Adults Can be Educated," in *Invitation to Lifelong Learning*, ed. Ronald Gross (Chicago: Follett, 1982), 99.

3. Betty Smith, *A Tree Grows in Brooklyn*, 14.

4. Mortimer J. Adler and Charles van Doren, *How to Read a Book* (New York: Touchstone, 1972), 115.

5. Ibid., 32–36.

6. Quoted in Clifton Fadiman, *The Lifetime Reading Plan* (Cleveland, Ohio: World, 1960), 28.

7. Dorothy L. Sayers and Jill Patton Walsh, *Thrones, Dominations* (New York: St. Martin's, 1998), 310.

8. Hurston, *Their Eyes Were Watching God*, 72.

9. Chaim Potok, *My Name Is Asher Lev* (New York: Fawcett Columbine, 1996), 291.

10. White, *Once and Future King*, 214.

11. Roger Lancelyn Green, *King Arthur and His Knights of the Round Table* (London: Puffin, 1994), 61.

12. Lee R. Steiner, *Where Do People Take Their Troubles?* (Boston: Houghton Mifflin, 1945).

13. Job 12:13.

14. Marshall, *Christy*, 175.

Chapter 13: Rhythm: Work and Rest

1. Anthony Trollope, *An Autobiography* (Oxford: Oxford University Press, 1999).

2. Ibid., 118–19.

3. Lindbergh, *Hour of Gold, Hour of Lead*, 130.

4. Mihaly Csikszentmihalyi, *Finding Flow* (New York: BasicBooks, 1997), 26.

5. Cather, *Song of the Lark*, 251.

6. Woolf, *A Writer's Diary*, 84.

7. Curie, *Madame Curie*, 143.

8. Didion, *Last Thing He Wanted*, 35.

9. Ralph Waldo Emerson, "Conduct of Life: Wealth," in *Complete Essays and Other Writings of Ralph Waldo Emerson*, 708.

10. Anne Lamott, *Traveling Mercies* (New York: Pantheon Books, 1999), 247.

11. Mihaly Csikszentmihalyi, *Creativity* (New York: HarperCollins, 1996), 138.

12. James Hillman, "Perambulate to Paradise," *Utne Reader*, March–April 2000, 86–89.

13. Brenda Ueland, *If You Want to Write* (St. Paul, Minn.: Graywolf, 1987), 33–34.

14. Jan Karon, *A Light in the Window* (Colorado Springs: Lion, 1995), 188.

15. Anne Morrow Lindbergh, *Gift from the Sea* (New York: Pantheon, 1955), 16.

16. Raymond Chandler, *The Lady in the Lake*, in *Later Novels and Other Writings* (New York: Library of America, 1995), 134.

17. Exod. 20:9–10.

Chapter 14: Action

1. Bellow, *Herzog*, 66.
2. Greene, *Heart of the Matter*, 194.
3. Luke 10:25.
4. 1 Peter 1:13.
5. Esther 4:14.
6. Prov. 14:8.
7. Fitzgerald, *Tender Is the Night*, 321.
8. Kent Haruf, *The Tie That Binds* (New York: Holt, Rinehart, and Winston, 1984), 148.
9. Jer. 6:16.
10. Sullivan, *Empress of One*, 4.
11. Elizabeth Alden Green, *Mary Lyon and Mount Holyoke*, 26.
12. Lindbergh, *Hour of Gold, Hour of Lead*, 215.

Chapter 15: The Conclusion of the Matter

1. I Kings 4:29.
2. I Kings 10:24.
3. Eccles. 8:16–17.
4. Eccles. 8:17.
5. Lewis, *Till We Have Faces*, 308.
6. Eccles. 12:13.
7. Eccles. 5:7.
8. Heb. 10:10.
9. Dostoevsky, *Brothers Karamazov*, 21.
10. Isa. 40:13–14.
11. Saint Augustine, *The Confessions*, trans. Maria Boulding (New York: Vintage Spiritual Classics, 1998), 72–73.
12. Isa. 6:3.
13. Hurston, *Their Eyes Were Watching God*, 151.

Nancy J. Nordenson is a freelance writer with a specialty in medical writing. She has written on a wide variety of medical topics for physicians, nurses, and other health care professionals, as well as for attorneys and health care consumers. She has also written for *Discipleship Journal* and *Focus on the Family*. She is a member of the American Medical Writers Association, American Society of Clinical Pathology, Minnesota Writers Guild, and the Loft Literary Center. Married with two sons, Nancy lives in Minneapolis.